WHITSONS WAY

The History of Whitsons Culinary Group®

A Story Rooted in Faith, Family, and Food

PAUL KING

with Jenny Dee

Whitsons Way

Copyright ©2024 Ginel, Inc
In Collaboration with Paul King and Jenny Dee

All rights reserved. The text of this publication, or any part thereof, may not be reproduced in any manner whatsoever without written permission from the publisher or authors.

Cover by Chelsea Yolalan
Cover Photo by Romariolen/iStock via Getty Images

Print ISBN: 978-1-954687-18-9
Ebook ISBN: 978-1-954687-19-6
Printed in the United States of America
First Edition

Published by Ginel, Inc.
1800 Motor Parkway
Islandia, NY 11749
www.whitsons.com

DISCLAIMER: The information presented in this book is for historical and informational purposes only. While every effort has been made to ensure the accuracy of the content at the time of publication, the authors and publisher disclaim any responsibility for errors or omissions. The content of this book has been derived from historical records, interviews with family members, and other sources believed to be reliable. The authors have tried to recreate events, locales, timelines, and conversations from interviews of first-hand recollections, though they are not written to represent word-for-word transcripts. Rather, the authors have retold them in a way that evokes the feeling and meaning of what was said.

Certain details have been omitted or anonymized to protect the privacy of individuals. The views expressed herein are those of the authors and of those interviewed and do not necessarily reflect the views of Whitsons Culinary Group or its affiliates. The authors and publisher shall not be liable for any loss, damage, or injury arising from the use of or reliance on the information provided in this book.

Trade names used herein are the property of their respective owners.

All book proceeds will be donated to the Whitsons Family Foundation to help Whitsons' team members in need.

Dedication

This book is dedicated to Elmer and Gina Whitcomb, who, in the middle of raising their family, took a major risk by starting a business with their children. The purchase of an existing restaurant in Garden City, NY, was a leap of faith that would change the trajectory of our entire family, impact the lives of many people, and help shape an entire industry. Thank you, Mom and Pop!

In Memoriam

In memory of Laurie Whitcomb Smith, our beloved sister.
Not a day goes by that we don't miss your joyful spirit.

We also remember all those team members we've lost along the way. We honor their service, their courage, and their impact on our lives. May they continue to rest in peace while their memories live on in our hearts.

In Gratitude for Our Team Members

This book was written for our team members past, present, and future.

This story is a testament to the power and legacy of the outstanding team members who have joined us on this journey throughout the last 45 years. We have been blessed to attract talented and caring people who have dedicated their careers to fulfilling Whitsons' mission and making a difference in the communities they serve.

Every team member is a part of our extended family. These are not just people who work for a company; they are extraordinary individuals who are deeply connected to our mission and do not hesitate to go above and beyond to satisfy customers, solve problems, and contribute to the team's overall success.

It does not matter whether they work on the front line, in the kitchen, on the road, as part of the corporate office team, or as an executive—we value each individual's contribution, as it takes many parts to make the whole a success. Our team members exemplify everything Whitsons stands for, and we would not be here today without their passion, commitment, and loyalty.

To all our team members: Thank you for putting your heart and soul into building Whitsons Way. We love you and are deeply grateful to you for sharing your lives with us.

Table of Contents

Introduction: A Mother's Pride

by Gina Whitcomb-Daly

When Elmer and I started this business in 1979, we couldn't have imagined in our wildest dreams that the company would grow to this size. Elmer simply had a plan to give his children a business of their own—that was what he wanted to leave as his legacy. He had been a mechanical engineer for 29 years, but he had a wonderful business sense and knew he could start his own business. He clearly passed that "can-do" attitude on to our children. He taught them well, and they listened. Before he passed, at only 57 years old, I asked him if he wanted to leave any advice or instructions about the business. But he said no, that Whitsons was in good hands, and he was sure we would succeed.

We didn't have an initial plan to get into the foodservice business. Elmer looked at many different business opportunities. We settled on food because it was a big thing in our family. Feeding our family with nine children was a big job; eventually, we realized it was the right choice for us.

Now, after all these years, I know our entire Whitsons "family" feels good about providing a service that helps people in a very personal way. I appreciate that, together, we have built a company whose team members genuinely enjoy serving our customers and making them feel happy and satisfied.

When we first started, it was just our three oldest sons, Bill, Doug, and Bob, who worked full-time at the Bon-Bon in Garden City. They had all graduated from college and worked in other businesses, but they liked their dad's idea of starting a business and working with each other. The others all helped out, too, and as each of our children graduated from college, they expanded their roles in the company to full-time, and it's worked incredibly well for them.

Everyone worked long, hard hours in the beginning. I baked a lot of cakes and pies for the shops in those days. But nobody seemed to mind because we were building something special. We moved into foodservice management, serving the Traveler's Insurance Company. They relocated a few years later, and then the Automobile Association of America (AAA) moved in, and the business just grew and grew from there. Now, with close to 5,000 team members and $500 million in sales, I'm not quite sure this was ever what Elmer had expected. I don't think he had foreseen how many others would become involved or the depth of success we would experience together—though he would never have doubted it.

The business has been a blessing for me. There was nothing more joyful for me than to come to work every day to see my children and our extended family of team members successfully working together. That was one of the reasons Elmer wanted to start the business—to keep our family together—and I am so happy that it worked. As fortunate as we've been, I can't say I am surprised.

Today, many of my sons have since retired, and my beloved daughter Laurie has passed, but each of them has left an indelible mark on my heart and the world. I am so proud of what they have accomplished together. I know that their father would be extremely proud of them as well. I'm sure he's in Heaven smiling down at them—and at every one of our team members.

My gratitude goes out to all of our team members for your years of support, hard work, and brilliant ideas that have helped to shape our company. Without each one of you, whatever your role may be, we would not be the company we are today. So, on behalf of Elmer, myself, and the entire Whitcomb family, thank you for so many wonderful years. May the future be just as successful as my husband and I dreamed it could be.

As Elmer always said: “It all starts with family.” And our family continues to grow—it lives on through all of you, our dear team members.

We hope our readers enjoy this inside look into Whitsons' humble beginnings and the love and sacrifice that went into making it the extraordinary company it is today. We have truly been blessed.

With Love and Gratitude,

Gina

The Whitcomb Family
Top Row: Bill, Doug, Bob, Mike, Andy
Bottom Row: Beth, Elmer, John, Gina, Paul, Laurie
***photo from family archives*

1.
A Business is Born

The year 1979 was historically noteworthy for any number of reasons. Margaret Thatcher was elected prime minister of Great Britain, the first woman ever to hold that post. The Iranian Revolution brought the Ayatollah Khomeini to power in that Middle Eastern country early in 1979, and students would later that year storm the US Embassy in Teheran and take 63 Americans hostage.

On March 28, the nuclear reactor at the Three Mile Island power plant in central Pennsylvania approached meltdown after a fire broke out in a cooling tower, making it the worst commercial nuclear disaster in US history. Karol Wojtyla, the Polish cardinal who had become Pope John Paul II the previous fall, returned to Poland, becoming the first pope to visit a Communist country. The U.S.S.R. invaded Afghanistan, the NFL's Pittsburgh Steelers won their record third Super Bowl, and the Sony Walkman was introduced.

But for the family of Elmer Whitcomb of Huntington, NY, on Long Island, there was only one date and one event that year that mattered. January 4, 1979, was the day the Whitcombs took possession of the 160-seat Bon-Bon restaurant on Franklin Avenue in Garden City, NY.

Elmer, who had recently retired from a career as a mechanical engineer with Sperry Gyroscope, had operated side businesses before, but the Bon-Bon would be different. This wasn't going to be a hobby. This was to be a new livelihood and, as such, would be a gamble—and a significant one at that.

Elmer and his wife Gina had sunk their entire life savings into the restaurant. The purchase of the Bon-Bon was the 52-year-old patriarch's calculated effort to bind his children—seven boys and two girls, ranging in age at the time from 27 to 7—to a common goal by creating a family business. The oldest boys had already begun to go their separate ways, following their own geography, and Elmer feared the effects of a fractured family. His hope was that his children would take this venture and make it a success and that the family would grow closer as a result.

So that first morning, well before the sun had even begun to brighten the horizon, Elmer and Gina, along with their second-oldest son, Doug, and his wife, Diane, entered the coffee shop and met the restaurant's 13 employees—seven waitresses, a chef, two short-order cooks, two counter persons, and a dishwasher.

They watched, learned, and assisted as the kitchen crew brought in the bread delivery, sliced the bagels, brewed the coffee, set out the pastries, cleaned and chopped the lettuce and other vegetables, made the salads, and began preparing the soups and other menu items for the day.

The Whitcombs knew precious little about management and nothing about running a restaurant, so their learning curve would be steep and not easy. Just how challenging would become evident all too quickly.

By the end of that first week, the Whitcombs had learned several unpleasant facts. Although the restaurant was open for breakfast, lunch, and dinner, virtually all of the business was done at lunch, and despite the new owners' best marketing efforts, that would never change. Revenue wasn't quite as robust as they had hoped, and the employees, all of them holdovers from the former operators, had gotten used to doing things a certain way: practices that sometimes were actually counterproductive to the effective management of the restaurant.

By the end of the first month, the financial picture was becoming clear, and it wasn't pretty. The previous owners, the Whitcombs eventually would discover, had misrepresented the business as being much more lucrative than it actually was, and the Whitcombs had been so trusting as to take them at their word.

As a result, they overpaid considerably for the Bon-Bon. These issues were compounded a year later when the Whitcombs took possession of a second restaurant literally a block away from the Bon-Bon, called the Blue Chip, from the same owners.

The two restaurants complemented each other in a sense: The Bon-Bon primarily served shoppers in the bustling downtown area, with a smattering of business people, while the Blue Chip's customers were mostly business people, along with the occasional shopper. (The Blue Chip's name reflected the traders working in nearby financial firms who made up much of the clientele.)

Each restaurant was similar to the other in that neither was destined to bring much to the family beyond heartache and painful life lessons.

To add a final indignity, two years into the business, Elmer was diagnosed with a very aggressive melanoma, starting on his neck and eventually metastasizing into his brain. He would be dead by the spring of 1984, and Gina and her children would need to pull together to somehow try to keep the failing restaurants afloat amid their grief.

This, then, is the history of a company that, by all conventional metrics, should not have survived its first decade.

Indeed, it was a miracle that the business had actually outlasted its founder. In fact, the firm not only survived, it eventually thrived, expanding from two financially challenging restaurants to a $500 million enterprise that not only manages foodservices for schools, institutions, and other accounts but also has created a successful prepared meals business with its own private label products.

Whitsons, as the company became known, has grown to close to 5,000 team members, and from its dual corporate headquarters on Long Island, New York, the company's reach stretches from Long Island, north to New England, west to central Illinois, and south to Florida, with more expansion on the horizon.

Much more than a simple chronology of events, the story of Whitsons is also a tale about the power of faith, the strength of family, the love of food, and the indomitable will of nine siblings for whom failure was simply not an option. And it all began with an only child for whom family became everything.

2.
From New England to Long Island

Elmer Whitcomb, the founder of what would become Whitsons Culinary Group, was born in Astoria, Queens, on May 18, 1927, the only child of Charles and Patricia Dornes Whitcomb. A couple of years later, the family moved to Bayside, Queens, where Elmer would live until he got married.

A private man, he never talked much with his children about his childhood. Paul, the youngest Whitcomb and the family's unofficial historian, notes that, in some ways, he knows more about the Whitcombs' ancestors than he does about his own father.

Although the Whitcombs' ancestry is a mix of English, Irish, Scandinavian, and German, Paul has been able to trace his family's direct lineage in the United States back to the Massachusetts Bay Colony shortly after the Pilgrims landed at Plymouth Rock. (Fun fact: during this research, it was uncovered that distant relatives of theirs were working for Whitsons in New England!)

Jonathan Whitcomb, originally of Taunton, England, immigrated to North America in 1655 and settled in Lancaster, the oldest settlement in what would become Worcester County in central Massachusetts. He and his wife, Hannah, had nine children, the youngest of which, John, would sire a Revolutionary War hero. That son, also named John, was born in 1711. He fought in the French and Indian War, beginning as a lieutenant and rising to the rank of lieutenant colonel.

By the time the colonies decided to secede from England, John had become a colonel in the Lancaster Minutemen. In 1775, he was commissioned as the first major-general of the Massachusetts

Army by the Third Provincial Congress and fought at the Battle of Bunker Hill. The following year, General George Washington commissioned him as a brigadier general in the Continental Army.

But the family discovered that General John wasn't the only Whitcomb of notoriety during these times. A generational cousin of John, Benjamin Whitcomb was also a well-known military leader, beginning as a soldier in the French and Indian War in 1754. He then went on to serve as a second lieutenant and worked his way up the ranks to lieutenant, captain commander, and, ultimately, major.

Most notably, during his tenure, Benjamin was given command of two companies of rangers, infamously dubbed "Whitcomb's Rangers," in 1776 (the same year John was appointed brigadier general). Benjamin would go on to lead the successful charges of his rangers scouting and protecting the North for many years as part of the Continental Army.

While the military prowess of both ancestors is evident in historical records, what is most remarkable for the Whitcomb family is the folklore of their tenacity and resilience throughout the warfare, alleged capture and release stories, and near-miss executions. Major Whitcomb surpassed all odds on the battlefield, dying peacefully in his sleep at the age of 91. General John would also pass in the same manner in his home at 72.

The Whitcomb Family Coat of Arms Illustrated by Charles E. Whitcomb (Elmer's father) in 1950

Over the decades after the United States achieved its independence, Whitcombs spread throughout New England and down into New York City. In the late 1800s, Elmer's grandfather, James—a direct descendant of General John—was the head of a noteworthy family in Astoria, a village in northwest Queens.

According to published accounts, James M. Whitcomb ran a livery stable in Astoria and was highly respected in the community by people of all races. It is indicative of his stature that when he died in 1904, the *Daily Star* (the local newspaper) printed a eulogy by one J. F. Rankin, a local citizen who called James, among other things, "a champion of equal rights."

Elmer's father, Charles E. Whitcomb, was an artist who specialized in airbrushing. Working primarily on a freelance basis, Charles retouched photos and illustrations for several magazines, including *Esquire* and *Harper's Bazaar*.

He also was an inventor of some renown. Among the patents he received were for a foldable desk, an enhanced system for moving puppets from below the stage, and the wall-mounted nameplate panels that we still see today in many multi-tenant buildings.

Charles' knack for science and design was passed down to his son, as Elmer would demonstrate in his own career. Graduating from Bayside High School in 1943, Elmer enlisted in the Naval Air Corps, where he spent 22 months. During that time, he also attended Williams College in western Massachusetts. When World War II ended, Elmer opted out of the Navy and returned home to ponder the next phase of his life.

Gina Kriete, a student at Syracuse University in northern New York, was home in Bayside in the summer of 1946, working as a clerk in a bookstore, when she met Elmer. As Gina remembers it, Elmer caught her eye one day when he came in to buy a book. She mentioned noticing this attractive young man to a coworker, who, as it happened, had been friends with Elmer since childhood.

The coworker introduced Elmer to Gina. The couple hit it off almost immediately, so much so that when Elmer decided to take some classes at Columbia University in Manhattan, Gina chose to do the same. However, Elmer wanted to become an engineer and ultimately believed that the University of Michigan would be the best place to help him achieve that goal. So, he matriculated to the Ann Arbor campus in 1947, and Gina visited him as often as she could.

Elmer pledged to the Sigma Nu fraternity, coincidentally at the same time as William A. Dart, who would go on to found Dart Container Corp., the original manufacturer of the polystyrene coffee cup. This was noteworthy because Elmer would later cite Dart as one of the friends whose success inspired him to take a chance on the Bon-Bon restaurant.

In June 1950, Elmer graduated from Michigan with a degree in mechanical engineering. But he wasn't on campus to attend commencement exercises and receive his diploma because he was back in New York preparing for another ceremony—his and Gina's wedding on July 1. He never went back to pick up his sheepskin; Paul eventually wrote to the university and had the diploma mailed to the house.

Elmer and Gina's marriage was an unusual union for the time period because Elmer was an Episcopalian, and Gina was Roman Catholic. Gina's mother was very strong in her faith, and one of her aunts was a Benedictine nun who eventually became the Mother Superior of a convent in Elizabeth, NJ.

Gina embraced their spirituality, and when she and Elmer were wed, she made only one request of him: that he allow their children to be raised Catholic. And it wasn't long before he had to honor that promise, as the couple wasted little time starting what would become a family of eleven.

Living in an apartment in Bayside, they had their first child, Bill, in 1951. Doug was born a year later, followed by Bob, John, Laurie, Mike, Andy, Beth, and finally, Paul in 1971.

When the oldest boys were little, Gina would go to Mass by herself, and Elmer would stay home to babysit. As the children grew, both in age and in number, Gina would take the older ones to church while Elmer stayed home with the younger ones.

Then, one day, out of the blue, Elmer told Gina that he wanted to attend Mass with the rest of the family. Before long, he decided to convert and received his Confirmation privately with his son Andy. As with many religious converts, Elmer became very passionate about his faith, and his newfound spirituality would play a critical role in the creation of the family business.

Elmer worked as a civil engineer in the Manhattan office of Babcock and Wilcox, a Charlotte, NC, energy company. It wasn't the type of engineering he was trained for, and he certainly wasn't thrilled with the commute, but his father-in-law had secured him the job, and it paid the bills as the Whitcomb family grew.

By the time Gina was pregnant with their third son, Bob, the Whitcombs knew it was time to buy their own house. Like many young families living on Long Island in that era, Elmer and Gina purchased their home in Levittown, a planned community in Nassau County conceived by Abraham Levitt and his sons, William and Alfred. The Whitcombs sold their Buick for $1,000 and used the money as a down payment.

They lived in Levittown for about a year before buying a house in Garden City. At about that same time, Elmer was hired by Sperry Gyroscope, an electronics company in Lake Success, about six miles northwest of Garden City. He worked for Sperry, which was primarily a government contractor, until he retired in 1979.

As befit his private nature—and no doubt due in part to the fact that his job gave him top-secret government clearance—Elmer didn't talk much about his work. "I knew he worked on gyros," Gina recalled, "and he loved his work. But when he came home, business was over, and he was with us."

His secrecy certainly wasn't CIA-level; the family knew, for example, about the trips he made to the White Sands Missile Range in New Mexico, and he would sometimes bring items home from the office to show the children. Eldest son Bill remembers his father coming home one evening with a laser, which he used to explode a red balloon inside a white balloon to demonstrate how a laser worked.

However, for the most part, Elmer preferred to leave work at the office, and it would be only over time that the family would learn, and be proud of, exactly what their father's job entailed.

Most facts were revealed by happenstance, or because of research Paul did. For example, Paul recalled a trip he and his sister Beth made with their parents to the Smithsonian Institution in Washington, DC, when Paul was 10.

"We were in the Air and Space Museum, and Dad showed me the lunar excursion module. He pointed to a box on the side and said, 'You see that box right there? Me and my team, we made that.' It was the gyroscopic guidance system for the LEM." Gina, reminded of the trip, recalled that it was the first time she knew her husband had anything to do with the Apollo space program.

Years after Elmer's death, as Paul was sifting through his father's possessions, he came across a couple of intriguing items. One was a plaque from the Secretary of the Navy, which recognized Elmer's role in developing the guidance system for the Polaris missile, the first ballistic missile launched from a submarine.

Although Bill remembers his father being on the USS George Washington when the missile system was tested in July of 1960, the plaque itself wasn't displayed anywhere the family could see it, and so the younger family members were unaware of the significance of their father's work.

The second item was what appeared to be a tie tack with the image of Snoopy, the beagle from the *Peanuts* comic strip, wearing a full space suit and helmet. Paul asked a friend to research the pin. The man discovered that the item was actually the Silver Snoopy Award, usually given to NASA employees and civilian contractors.

After the tragic Apollo 1 fire that killed astronauts Gus Grissom, Roger Chaffee, and Ed White, NASA officials felt they needed a symbol that employees could rally behind to promote safety in the space program. NASA approached Charles Schulz about using Snoopy, who not only was a well-known character in comics but was a "flier" himself; one of the storylines in *Peanuts* was Snoopy's fantasy of his doghouse as a World War I Sopwith Camel battling the dreaded Red Baron.

The award, still in existence, recognizes individuals who help promote safety and conscientiousness within the space program. Astronauts would fly Snoopy pins with them into space and then present them to selected workers after the mission. This award is coveted and given to less than 1% of the civilians who work with NASA.

The most amazing thing about the awards, according to Paul,

was that they were always presented in public ceremonies, and yet Gina had no idea her husband had received the award until Paul discovered it among his father's effects. That was, in Paul's words, "the way my dad was—focused on doing the right things, for the right reasons, and not for accolades. The more I learned about him, the more I discovered the depths of his humility."

Records do not indicate which astronaut presented the pin to Elmer, but it apparently came from the Apollo 7 mission, which was led by Wally Schirra. Paul also discovered, in his search of Elmer's possessions, that his dad had received a commendation from NASA as part of the "rate gyro anomaly team" that devised a solution to a gyroscopic problem aboard Skylab, the US' first space station, during its third mission in 1973.

But it wasn't just these hidden accomplishments that made Elmer different from most businessmen; it was his heart as a family man that truly made him special.

"He was a very devoted father. A very unselfish man," Gina recalls with love. "He was a disciplinarian, but in a nice way—in a way to teach our children the value of hard work and integrity. Of course, he was easier on his girls than he was on the boys. Oh, he was a gentleman through and through."

Daughter Laurie, now deceased, once shared, "There was a very warm side that not too many people got to see. He was one way in business and one way at home. As a little girl, I remember he was very warm and gentle."

Youngest daughter Beth also shared another unknown side to him: his sense of humor. When Elmer found something funny, he would apparently laugh, and his whole body would shake, starting a domino effect of laughter throughout the room. Paul shared that he was also a bit of a practical joker: "You never knew if what he said was the truth or a joke in those moments."

Elmer was the kind of man who could do anything, and he relished the chance to teach what he knew to all of the children. And by the time the Whitcombs had moved from Garden City to a house in Huntington Station, there was *a lot* for the kids to learn and do. The house was a 17-room structure that sat on three acres of land on East Rogues Path on the eastern side of the town.

Technically, it wasn't a farm, but by the time Elmer and Gina were done with it, it may have seemed like one. For a time, the Whitcombs raised and bred Saint Bernards for sale—one of which briefly became a TV celebrity.

In 1967, singer/songwriter John Sebastian, at the time lead singer for *The Lovin' Spoonful,* bought a Saint Bernard puppy from the Whitcombs. Sebastian, who lived on the eastern end of Long Island in Sag Harbor, was looking for a companion for his golden retriever. Although he no longer remembers all the details, he somehow learned of the Whitcombs' puppies and traveled over to Huntington Station. He chose one of the pups and named it Orpheus.

Two weeks later, *The Lovin' Spoonful* were set to make their third appearance on the Ed Sullivan Show. Sebastian said the producers wanted to try out some new technology whereby people and things could seem to appear and disappear on screen, as if by magic. (They were scheduled to sing their hit "Do You Believe In Magic?")

"Well, at one point in the song, they were going to have a go-go dancer appear," Sebastian recalled. "I didn't like that idea very much, so I said, 'What if we used a dog?'" The producers went with the idea, and 37 seconds into the group's performance, Orpheus got his two seconds of fame. (The video of the performance can be found on YouTube.)

In addition to the dogs, the property was home to cats, ducks, chickens, a horse, and a pony. At one point, the Whitcombs even owned two pigs, which were raised and then slaughtered for the meat.

"It wasn't a good investment, but it was a wonderful way to learn," Gina said. "Elmer told me, 'I want the children to experience everything. How do I know what the future holds for them? If they experience everything, they'll never be at a loss.'"

Being children, the young Whitcombs didn't always perform their animal husbandry duties properly. There were more than a few telephone calls from neighbors wanting to know if the family was aware that their horse or one of their pigs was wandering down East Rogues Path. One or more of the children would then have to get a rope and a bucket of food and try to lure the wayward animal back home.

The children seemed to develop their own individual talents based on genetics and/or their childhood experiences. Doug and Bob discovered early on that they, like Elmer, were mechanically inclined, and one day, they came home from Maplewood Elementary School pushing a Vespa 400.

The Vespa was an Italian car manufactured between 1956 and 1961. It was a tiny thing, only 9 feet long and weighing less than 800 pounds. The Vespa had a 2-cylinder, 2-stroke engine—mounted in the rear of the vehicle—with 14 horsepower and a top speed of 56 miles an hour. It was a convertible of sorts; the canvas roof could be rolled down like a tent flap. A teacher had donated the car to the boys, and they persuaded a few friends to help them get it home.

They managed to repair it and get it up and running, and that set them on the road to creating a small auto repair business when they were in high school. Elmer's parents, both of whom were very artistic, even made a sign for the boys to post along the side of the road by the house. The advertisement was short-lived—the town ordered the Whitcombs to remove it because it violated a local zoning ordinance.

Bob recalls that there were parallels between the auto repair business and the early years at the restaurants; in particular, the boys were flying by the seat of their pants, gaining knowledge with each new job.

"People would come up the driveway, and they would say, 'Can you fix my car?' and I'd say, 'Sure.' If I didn't know how, I learned as I went along. I knew the basics of tune-ups and brake jobs. One guy came to me and said he wanted me to rebuild his engine. So, I learned how to do that. I learned never to say 'no' to a customer... and I carried that philosophy with me throughout my life."

Sometimes, the lessons came the hard way, fortunately never with any serious consequences. Bob remembers doing a brake job for a classmate, only to have his friend return two days later with his tires thumping and wobbling.

Bob had neglected to apply the proper torque to the wheels' lug nuts, and they had come loose. Bob was able to secure the bolts properly without his friend realizing what had happened. Oblivious, he thanked Bob profusely for being so quick to diagnose and solve the problem. In 2011, at Bob's 40-year high school reunion, he ran into his classmate and finally confessed the true story.

Sometimes, it was not always immediately evident to family members the source of a particular talent. For example, Bill is very musically inclined and played in rock and roll bands in the late 60s and early 70s. His ability came from Elmer, who was an accomplished pianist—not that many people were aware of it.

For years, only Gina knew, understanding that Elmer's virtuosity clashed with his private nature. By the time he reached adulthood, he once told Gina, he had grown so tired of being trotted out by his parents to perform for guests at home or at some public function that he preferred that people not know of his talent. So, even though the Whitcombs owned a piano, Elmer would play only if he thought no one was around to hear. If someone entered the room, he immediately would stop playing.

Except, of course, when it came to his children.

"When we were very young, he used to play the piano for us. He was something else. Those moments are among my most special memories," says Bill.

Bill, although he inherited his father's musical ability, did not possess Elmer's shyness. As a teenager, Bill hoped that he might one day make his living as a musician. But that never came to pass.

Andy's artistic bent came out in another way, one that would serve him well in the family business. He had a natural curiosity about food. He was the one most likely to want to experiment with unfamiliar kinds of foods. Andy recalls that there wasn't a lot of culinary variety in the Whitcomb household, so he began to explore cuisines on his own.

In high school, Andy opted for vocational training and took two years of culinary classes. His first job, at the Huntington Bay Yacht Club, opened his eyes to the camaraderie and the competition of the kitchen, and he found that he felt most at home in that environment.

"I couldn't have asked for my family to choose a better business for me to be a part of. It's brought me a personal fulfillment that I cannot imagine from any other profession," reflects Andy.

The other children were touched in other ways. Beth got her love of numbers and finance from Grandpa Kriete, who was an accountant. She went to college to study accounting and might have gone on to law school if there had been no family business, perhaps to specialize in corporate law.

More than the other children, John's and Mike's hearts and desires were shaped by the family's spiritual nature. John studied social work in college, and Mike spent three years in the late 1980s in a Catholic seminary and is now a deacon. Paul found that he had a knack for persuasion, which served him well when he joined his brother Doug on the sales force at Whitsons.

The children all learned about business from an early age; specifically, if you wanted something, you had to earn it. For example, if one of the boys wanted to buy a go-kart, Elmer would have that son sign a contract that spelled out exactly what tasks he would have to do in order to earn the go-kart. These jobs were in addition to the regular chores they were expected to perform after school and on Saturday mornings.

"My dad was very precise," Andy reveals. "A stickler for detail and doing things himself. He was always hands-on and raised us to be the same. He never allowed people to take that ability and experience away from him. It's what sparked his creativity."

Paul says that one of his strongest memories was "being forced to work. I remember some clashes over having to mow the lawn, rake the leaves, stack the wood, or perform some other chore I didn't want to do. While I resented it growing up, I now appreciate those lessons far more than I ever thought.

"I just wanted to have fun, like most kids do, but Dad used these opportunities to teach us about the value of hard work and responsibility. We were a kind of do-it-yourself family. If we needed more space at the house, we added a room. If we needed furniture, we built it. If a car was broken, we would fix it.

"I don't know if it was out of necessity or if Dad intentionally took on all this additional work just to teach us how to be self-sufficient. What I do know is that I didn't appreciate what he was doing when he was doing it, but as a parent, I can now see the wisdom in his actions and the love and commitment that they required."

Beth also remembers the chores. "Raking was my least favorite. With three acres, you can imagine how much there was to do." But she also remembers the warmth and closeness of the family. Everyone was together for dinner every night except when Elmer was traveling. After dinner, Gina would read a passage from the Bible, and the family would discuss it before praying the rosary.

"Dinnertime was fun," said Beth. "We had a long table, and there were benches because you couldn't fit enough chairs around. Food wasn't scarce, but because there were all these boys around—hungry wrestlers—you had to get your food quickly, or it wasn't going to be there."

Wrestling was both an indoor and outdoor sport for the Whitcombs. It might start in the living room with two boys, but it often quickly tumbled out into the front yard with the four oldest going at it full tilt. Clothes would be torn, and knees would become grass-stained.

Eventually, the older boys were able to release their energy by joining their schools' wrestling teams, and from that experience was born a competitive spirit—and an ability to learn from their failures—that would one day give them the edge they needed to succeed in the business world.

"Wrestling taught us a lot," Doug explained. "Wrestling may be a team sport, but it's still an individual event, you against your opponent. Whether your hand is raised or not, you stand all alone and process what happened. When you lose, you have to decide how you're going to handle it."

"There's not a successful wrestler who hasn't figured out how to learn from failure," agrees John. "You can't be successful as a wrestler unless you can problem solve and overcome loss. There is an encyclopedia of lessons there, and no one can teach them to you. You have to figure them out."

Even though he was an engineer by profession, Elmer also had a head for business and an entrepreneurial spirit that was fueled in part by seeing several of his friends—such as his fraternity brother Bill Dart—go into business for themselves and become successful.

The Whitcombs already had the side business breeding

Saint Bernards, but in 1969, Elmer bought a small laundromat in Levittown. Gina managed the day-to-day operation, interacting with customers, while Elmer would spend evenings and weekends repairing machines as necessary and handling the finances. Eventually, Elmer sold that business and purchased a larger laundromat in Huntington Village. There, the older boys, Bob in particular, would work after school, washing and folding customers' laundry and helping Elmer fix washers and dryers.

"My father inculcated an entrepreneurial spirit in us from the beginning," said Bob, "and trained us to serve the public with our experience in the laundromats.

"What was most interesting was his ability to read what customers wanted. He was a very technically smart, analytical, and intelligent man—but he was an extremely shy person by nature. By all accounts, he was not well-suited personality-wise to being in businesses that served the public, and yet he knew the importance of customer service and taught us about it."

It all comes back to Elmer's innate humble nature, which was meant to serve but from behind the scenes.

Gina once confided to Paul that his father had ample opportunities for advancement at Sperry, which he always turned down because the increase in required traveling would have meant too much time away from his family. Elmer made it clear that family would always be more important to him than his career.

So, in the mid-1970s, as the oldest boys reached their teenage years and beyond, Elmer became concerned about what seemed to be an inevitability: soon, the tight-knit family was going to break up. Bill had left home at 18 and was traveling the world, living by his wits and experiencing myriad adventures.

Doug, having graduated from Auburn University in Alabama, was married to Diane and living in Georgia. John was attending college in Connecticut. Bob was married to MaryLou and living in an apartment above MaryLou's grandparents' home in Huntington Station.

Elmer feared that it was only a matter of time before Bob also would seize the opportunity to spread his wings. Elmer wanted to keep his family close, and in his mind, there was only one way to do that.

So, Elmer decided to retire from Sperry and write a new chapter in his life. He told his wife: "Engineering I cannot give them. The only thing I can give my children is a business, and I know how to run a business. I can write business proposals."

Soon, he would draft the proposal that would change the lives of the entire family.

3.
We Bought a Restaurant

In the summer of 1977, Elmer and Gina made the decision to invest their life savings in a family business. Elmer would cash in his life insurance policy, along with his pension from Sperry, and would take out a second mortgage on the family home. Now, all they had to do was settle on a business they thought they could afford and manage successfully.

The older boys had various reactions to the news. Bill was enjoying his life as a globe-trotter and wasn't quite prepared to settle down. Doug, on the other hand, was excited at Elmer's decision. Living in Georgia was fun, but he missed New York, which, in his mind, would always be home. So, he and his wife Diane packed up and made the move back to Long Island.

John, who was attending Southern Connecticut State University in New Haven, was ambivalent. He loved his family, but he liked Connecticut and planned to live there and become a social worker after graduation. Bob, attending Hofstra University on Long Island, was firmly committed to the family's plan. As it would turn out, he would graduate and take a job with an insurance firm before the family business was born.

But all of them, to one degree or another, aided in the search for the right enterprise.

Before the project could begin in earnest, Elmer thought he needed some additional guidance. Specifically, the Catholic convert wished for a sign from God that he was making the right choice. It was Gina who supplied the medium. She sometimes visited a retreat house in Somers, CT, and it was through friends she'd met there that she was put in touch with Sister Bertrand, a cloistered Dominican nun who lived in the Monastery of Our Lady of Grace in North Guilford.

"Sr. Bertrand had the ability to read souls," Gina said. "People from all over—priests, bishops, everybody—came to see her. She was just very spiritual, a very holy nun."

So, Elmer and Gina made the trip to Connecticut with the younger children, picking up John from SCSU along the way so that Elmer could seek Sr. Bertrand's guidance. As Gina remembered it, as the group made their way down the main hallway of the monastery, Sr. Bertrand approached them from the other direction.

Without knowing exactly why the Whitcombs had come to see her, the nun took one look at the group and said, "What a lovely family for a family business." That was all Elmer needed to hear. As far as he was concerned, his wish had been granted; his endeavor was blessed by a higher power.

For more than a year, the family would scan newspaper ads, searching for businesses for sale. Their weekends were spent traveling, sometimes as far as Boston, to view potential targets—motels, bed and breakfasts, restaurants, even a meat packing plant, and a towing company—whatever they thought might be a good fit and could involve all of the family members.

Their evenings were spent doing the financial analysis of each prospect, as well as weighing the business's location versus the family's desire to stay in the New York City metro area. In the end, they settled on a restaurant on Franklin Avenue in nearby Garden City called the Bon-Bon.

Garden City has the distinction of being one of the country's first planned communities. It was founded in 1869 by millionaire Alexander Turney Stewart, who made his fortune selling Irish linens and lace goods.

Stewart purchased 10,000 acres on the Hempstead Plains to create his vision of an idyllic village and incorporated the Central Railroad of Long Island to shuttle residents between Garden City and Long Island City, which is across the East River from Manhattan. When Stewart died in 1876, his wife Cornelia continued his work, and when she passed away in 1886, the Stewarts' heirs led the

Garden City Company to further development.

Today, Franklin Avenue in Garden City is home to a plethora of eateries of all types. There are Asian and Italian restaurants, sushi, tapas, oyster, and wine bars, pizza and sandwich joints, and the ubiquitous Starbucks, among others. But in 1979, there were only a handful of restaurants in the area. Two of them, the Bon-Bon and the Blue Chip, were a block apart, and Howard and Esther Bassoff of nearby Mineola owned them both.

During their negotiations with the Whitcombs, the Bassoffs indicated that both restaurants were available. The Whitcombs, unfamiliar with the restaurant business, thought they might have more success if they controlled their closest competitor. So, they agreed to purchase the Bon-Bon for $450,000, with an option to buy the Blue Chip in a year's time for $250,000.

Imbued with their faith and old-fashioned enough to take people at their word, the Whitcombs thus made the first of many mistakes of which they would be guilty over the next few years. As it turned out, the Bassoffs had misrepresented the restaurants, both in terms of what they were worth and the revenue they generated.

As a result, Doug later learned that the Whitcombs overpaid for the Bon-Bon by a factor of four and for the Blue Chip by a factor of three. The new owners started business in a hole out of which they seemed destined never to climb.

(Although the Whitcombs never pursued any legal action against the Bassoffs, in 2007, Esther Bassoff pleaded guilty to grand larceny and scheming to defraud in a case involving another of the Bassoffs' business dealings. According to records from the New York State Supreme Court, Bassoff was given five years' probation and ordered to pay $175,000 in restitution.)

But the Whitcombs were fully committed to the venture. Elmer and Gina had assembled all the money they could muster in order to bring Elmer's vision to life. And so on Thursday, January 4, 1979, before dawn on what would be a cold but clear day in Garden City, Elmer and Gina, along with Doug and Diane, stood on Franklin Avenue outside the Bon-Bon.

The family took a deep breath and stepped inside the 160-seat coffee shop, where their new professional life beckoned. Staff welcomed them enthusiastically but briefly, for there was work to be done. Nearly 45 years later, Doug's memory of that day was still fresh.

"It was a day filled with extraordinary exuberance and a measure of deep concern," he recalled. "And there was even fear for all the things we didn't understand. We approached the day like all people who don't know what lies ahead, with a hope and a dream that we could make things better."

The Bon-Bon occupied a long rectangular building down the west side of Franklin Avenue, between 9th Street and Stewart Avenue, and across the street from an A & S department store.

The restaurant's dark brown color scheme was affected by pecky cypress paneling, decorated in a Norman Rockwell motif by Elmer and Gina—"If it graced the cover of the Saturday Evening Post, they probably had a version of it in the restaurant," said Doug. A long, curved counter with a white laminate top, lined with 24 stools, ran down the first half of the coffee shop. A soda fountain and a mix of booths and tables comprised the rest of what was visible to customers.

Among the 13 employees the Whitcombs inherited were a few workers Doug still remembers vividly. Helen, the waitress in charge of all the two tops, was "lightning on feet, capable of doing 20 things at once and still singing a song at the same time." Tommy, the counterman, knew his customers so well that he anticipated their orders and could get what they needed before they even thought to ask.

Joe, the dishwasher, a quiet man from the South, never missed a day of work, no matter the weather or what he might have been doing the night before. And he became more than a pot scrubber. He also helped the chef make several regular menu items, including rice pudding, one of many items for which the Bon-Bon became well known.

Breakfast business was typically modest, with about 10 to 30 customers per day. Many of them were regulars, like the dentist from down the street and the saleswoman who came in from Martin Trencher's, the dress shop next store. But lunch was always a rush, with tables usually turning three times.

"I remember having to open the Bon-Bon, cook the bacon, brew the coffee, and bake the muffins before I could open for business," recalls Bob. "I tried to get these chores completed early so I could enjoy a fresh roll and coffee before the first customer came in."

In 1979, Franklin Avenue was a bustling place where the locals usually shopped, and would remain that way until a major expansion of nearby Roosevelt Field Mall took place in 1993. Garden City at that time was known for several wedding dress shops, so it wasn't unusual for the Bon-Bon to have a wedding party come in after a fitting for a meal or a snack. Shoppers made up the bulk of the lunch crowd, along with a few businesspeople and the occasional celebrity.

Soap opera star Susan Lucci, who grew up in Garden City and still lives there, often came in on Saturdays with her family for hamburgers and milkshakes. Other famous regulars included actor Telly Savalas, who owned an apartment around the corner, and middleweight boxer Rocky Graziano.

In the early days of the business, the cast of family characters included Elmer, who worked mainly behind the scenes managing the books; Gina, who served as a cashier; Doug, who managed the restaurant; and his wife, Diane, who worked the floor as the hostess. In addition, Gina and Diane baked pies that were sold in the coffee shop.

Bill, whose wanderlust had been satisfied and was now working as a delivery driver for a window and door manufacturer in Middle Village, Queens, was pressed into service as a short-order cook two weeks after the family took over the eatery. Bob left his job at the insurance company and joined the family in the early spring of 1979. Mike left Nassau Community College and would grow in the business, "doing a little bit of everything."

John would join the company about a year later, after graduating from Southern Connecticut State, starting as a busboy and dishwasher. He remembers his early days, which shaped the course of his life, as if they were yesterday.

"We were working long hours—14 to 16 hours a day—with little time off, even on weekends, to do something we could all be proud of. It was a wonderful experience working with my parents and siblings to build something very special from scratch like that."

Laurie and Andy helped out at the Bon-Bon whenever and however they could. Andy would leave culinary school after Elmer died and meld into the business full-time.

Beth, the accountant, would play her part in helping with the bookkeeping end of the business. As Paul got older, he also would make his way to the Bon-Bon after school to bus tables or wash dishes. Of all the siblings, only Laurie, who died in 2007, never joined the enterprise full-time. However, two of Laurie's six children did enter the business and continue to work there today.

For Doug and Bob, in particular, as the company's "front men," the learning curve would necessarily be steep and treacherous. Aside from their brief stint as auto mechanics in high school, they had no experience running a business. Work was certainly not foreign to them; management, however, was.

Elmer, of course, understood business; he had operated the two laundromats successfully and sold them for a profit. But again, there were no employees to manage there. In addition, the family was stepping into a business with a notoriously high failure rate.

Although there are no firm statistics on the rate of closures among restaurants acquired by new owners (the Bon-Bon originally opened in the mid-1960s), according to data compiled by researchers at Ohio State University, slightly more than 60% of independently owned restaurants fail within the first year of operation. Of the ones that survive the initial 12 months, 70% are out of business within five years.

As things would shake out, the Whitcombs' lack of restaurant experience was both a hardship and a blessing. To their credit, they chose not to come in and make wholesale changes to personnel or the menu.

In addition to the rice pudding the Bon-Bon was known for, they decided to keep the house-made corned beef and its "bottomless" cup of coffee; the family was not about to change what seemed to work. Many of the employees had worked there for several years, and the Whitcombs wanted to maintain that continuity.

Of course, these "non-moves" were born of necessity because the family had more than enough on their plates just learning the ins and outs of the business: scheduling staff, managing people, processing invoices, and complying with health department regulations.

They had to understand the language of the waitstaff and the kitchen crew. They had to learn how to deal with the quirky nature of vendors, who often valued relationships over sales and could be quick to take advantage of anyone they felt was an easy mark.

When it came to inventory, there was a balancing act that had to be perfected: order too little of a product and you run the risk of running out of a popular menu item; order too much and the excess would either spoil before it was used or simply "walk" out of freezers or coolers.

The two most important lessons the young entrepreneurs learned in the first few weeks were, in Doug's words, "There is much more to the picture than what is visible" and "If you can't measure it, you can't manage it."

Everything, it seemed, would have to be learned by trial and error. Within days of taking over the Bon-Bon, the Whitcombs lost one of their short-order cooks. Doug stepped in and quickly came to understand that such people are a rare breed, able to keep multiple orders in their heads and time everything they were preparing down to the second so that, for example, all the orders for a particular table would be ready at the same time.

Doug didn't have that ability, so older brother Bill stepped into the kitchen fray and discovered that he was one of those precious few who were born to this type of work. "Billy could cut seconds into pieces and manage them," Doug marveled.

One challenge of purchasing an established restaurant is that it can be difficult to attract new customers, and that certainly seemed to be the case with the Bon-Bon. Also, the weekly revenue—$8,000—was barely enough to cover everyone's wages, pay vendors and utility companies, and meet the financial obligations of the promissory notes, issued at 8% interest by the Bassoffs.

As a result, the Whitcombs themselves worked for little or no pay for the first few years of operation. The headaches only multiplied in 1980, when the time came for the Whitcombs to exercise their option on the Blue Chip restaurant. Bob became the manager of the Blue Chip, leaving Doug to oversee the Bon-Bon.

The Blue Chip was similar to the Bon-Bon in terms of design and menu, but it needed a facelift more than its counterpart. The clientele also was different, with the Blue Chip serving mostly businesspeople. The Blue Chip generated less than $5,000 a week in revenue, and with two restaurants to pay off, money became tighter than ever.

With each billing cycle, the question had to be answered: Who would get paid, and who would have to wait? Sometimes, vendors were asked to be patient, and other times, the Bassoffs were made to wait. It wasn't unusual to have a utility company send someone—often at inopportune times, such as the lunch rush—to threaten the Whitcombs with shut-off unless at least a portion of a bill was paid.

John recalled "bouncing checks to the point where the local bank didn't want to do business with us."

With revenue from the two coffee shops pretty much fixed, reducing costs seemed to be the only viable option. For a couple of years, in an effort to control expenses and learn more about the purchasing side of the business, the Whitcombs decided to do their own shopping for meat, seafood, and produce at the 113-acre Hunt's Point Market in The Bronx.

"I learned the foundation of the industry working behind the counter and traveling to Hunts Point to pick out all of the produce for the restaurant," Andy remembered vividly. "It was quite the learning adventure."

Founded in 1929 and then expanded and modernized several times over the years, Hunt's Point is the world's largest produce market. At midnight each day, two or three family members would hop into Mike's pickup truck for the trip into the south Bronx, which at the time was the most crime-ridden spot in New York City's five boroughs—on one trip, they were robbed of all their cash before they could make a single purchase.

They would meet with vendors and negotiate deals on heads of lettuce, cauliflower, and broccoli; bushels of string beans, tomatoes, and onions; sides of beef; and fillets of fish. They would get what they needed and then return to Garden City in time to open the restaurant that morning, a grueling schedule that, in the end, really didn't do all that much to help the bottom line.

The experience was enlightening, if not exactly pleasant. The Whitcombs were small fry, rubbing elbows and butting heads with professional buyers who, sometimes, represented dozens of establishments.

The Whitcombs were willing to try almost anything to bring costs under control. At one point, they even went so far as to make their own syrups for their fountain drinks, which they did for a couple of years. They abandoned the practice as the company grew, and the industry moved away from soda fountains and more to canned and bottled beverages. But it further exemplified the do-it-yourself approach the family embraced.

Everything seemed to be working against the family. Six months into the business, an oil crisis reminiscent of the 1973 oil embargo struck, and the price of gasoline went from 34 cents a gallon to $1.50. The ensuing economic downturn hit banks hard, and interest rates soared.

Customers began watching their money more tightly, either by not spending as much or not coming to the restaurants as often. Even when the Whitcombs managed to make a successful move, fate would intervene to deal them a staggering blow.

Perhaps the most infamous example was when the Whitcombs were chosen to operate a restaurant in the new 450,000-square-foot Franklin Avenue Office Complex, which opened in early 1981. The complex, owned by the Pepitone family, consisted of four separate buildings. There was to be a centrally located restaurant in a basement space.

Doug approached the building managers and offered to run the restaurant. He was rebuffed initially, but when the owners' preferred choice of restaurateur backed out, they came back to the Whitcombs and asked them to step in. The challenge was two-fold: rent would be $12,000 a month, and the Whitcombs would have to build out the space—for which the family had little money.

So, being the self-reliant individuals that they were, Elmer and his sons retired to their garage and built whatever they could—

counters, tables, and the like. What they couldn't construct, they would buy at auctions. Running the restaurant, hitting Hunt's Point, and constructing tables and serving counters made for long days and sleepless nights for the older Whitcombs.

Even during the build-out of the new space, the family learned another painful lesson about trust. At an equipment auction, Elmer met a man named Richie Mammolito, and the two struck up a friendship.

Elmer decided to use Mammolito as their purchasing agent. He would buy items and bring them to the complex, and the Whitcombs would repay him. Eventually, Mammolito balked at using his own money upfront, and so the family gave him a $20,000 advance on equipment purchases. Mammolito promptly absconded with the money. The Whitcombs got a judgment against the man, but it was never satisfied.

Still, the Whitcombs were able to open their new restaurant, Ginel, as they referred to it (a melding of Gina's and Elmer's names) on time and to great success. It certainly helped that every available space in the complex, which was anchored by Dime Savings Bank, rented quickly.

Employees came to Ginel in droves, and the Whitcombs finally appeared to be on their way. So popular and profitable was Ginel that in 1986, another restaurateur offered the family $700,000 to take over the space. But the Whitcombs were sure they had a gold mine and turned down the offer.

"Ginel was very avant-garde for its time," shares Andy. "Our father built that place from scratch, everything from the counters to the serveries to the cashier stations. He was an industrious man who constantly took risks to support his family—and we really believed in this business."

But as with all risks, not every one of them pans out as expected, as was the case with Ginel. Six months later, Dime Savings Bank pulled out of the complex after a dispute with the landlord and moved to the new EAB Towers in Hempstead. Because Dime's employees represented half of Ginel's customer base, Ginel's sales plummeted. Worse, the Pepitones wouldn't lower Ginel's rent, and so this restaurant also became a losing proposition.

However, by this time, the Whitcombs had learned a thing or two about business dealings and contracts. Bob contacted the owners, who had just hired a new business manager. The manager agreed to sit down with Bob, who by this time was the head of what was then called Whitsons Industries.

During the conversation, the manager refused to budge from the negotiated rent figure. However, he agreed to modify the lease—more than likely because he felt there were some terms he could insert that would benefit him. However, one of the modifications was one that gave either party termination rights under certain circumstances.

Shortly after the new lease was executed, Bob informed the manager that Whitsons was invoking its right to terminate unless the rent was reduced to a more financially palatable level. The manager was shocked and embarrassed—but not so much that he would lower the rent. So, 30 days later, Whitsons was out of the Franklin Avenue Office Complex. That was the end of Ginel.

4.
Out of Tragedy, Purpose

No matter how many trials and tribulations Whitsons faced as a company in those early years, they were nothing when matched against the personal heartache the family suffered beginning in 1981 when Elmer was diagnosed with melanoma.

The cancer began as a mole on Elmer's neck. Gina urged her husband to see a dermatologist, but Elmer had never been a fan of doctors, and he kept putting off a visit. His hand was forced, however, when Gina's brother William died.

Because William had been a surgeon, there were a number of doctors at his wake. Gina asked one of them to look at Elmer's neck, and the doctor immediately suggested that the mole be examined by a specialist as quickly as possible. The growth was found to be malignant, and Elmer underwent surgery, during which the mole and a significant portion of the left side of Elmer's neck were removed. He then underwent chemotherapy, which kept the melanoma at bay for a time.

Elmer wasn't about to give up, so he continued working, helping to keep the restaurants' books and doing what he could to help his sons explore other foodservice options for the business.

But he also was pragmatic, and he knew the statistics about cancer and survival rates. Although the average survival rate for melanoma today is 90% or better, in the 1980s, the rate was about half of that. So, Elmer began spending more time with his younger children, particularly Paul and Beth.

Paul recalled taking a number of family trips in the early 1980s, including one to Niagara Falls and that illuminating visit to the nation's capital and the Air and Space Museum. But he and Beth didn't quite absorb the reason behind those adventures; they didn't understand just how ill their father was.

And Elmer did seem healthier for a time. In April 1982, Bob and his brothers convinced Elmer to lease a new Cadillac Fleetwood. It would be the first time he ever had owned a new car, and Elmer very nearly changed his mind before signing the papers. But Bob recalled the look of pride on his father's face when he drove that car home and showed it to Gina.

"This was a brief time for my dad to look good, feel good, enjoy his new car, and watch his boys fully engaged in the business," he said.

Unfortunately, that respite would fade much too quickly. By mid-1983, the melanoma had come back with a vengeance, metastasizing into other parts of Elmer's body, including his brain. Neither chemo nor radiation was effective any longer in fighting the cancer.

Elmer knew he was involved in a losing battle, and during a walk that fall with Gina, he looked at the trees and confided, "These might be the last leaves I ever see."

While he was being treated at Memorial Sloan Kettering Hospital on Manhattan's Upper East Side, Gina was at his side every day. To avoid the commute from Long Island, she would stay at the Sisters of Charity Convent near the hospital for up to two weeks at a time, a courtesy arranged by Father John McConnell, a Jesuit priest who was the brother of one of the Whitcombs' neighbors. Clinging to her faith despite the circumstances, Gina said the nuns were "God's way of getting me through all this."

It pained the family to see their father becoming weaker by the day. Elmer was their rock, their superhero, a man who relished challenges and always seemed to come out on top. And yet, here he was, being defeated by forces inside his own body. It was nearly unfathomable.

But Elmer refused to give up without a fight. Weak as he was, he still possessed an inner strength that he would demonstrate one day shortly before Christmas when, to the family's utter shock, he appeared on the front porch of their Huntington home. Elmer had signed himself out of Sloan Kettering on East 68th Street and made his way down to West 34th Street, where he caught the Long Island Railroad to Huntington Station. Then he walked home from the train station, a distance of just over a mile and a half.

"I'm not spending my last Christmas in the hospital," he told his wife when she met him at the door.

Elmer would live to see new leaves on the trees, but just barely. He never returned to Sloan Kettering. Eventually, in his last days, he was placed in Huntington Hospital. There, on April 17, 1984, with his family surrounding him and praying the rosary, Elmer Whitcomb died. He was only 57.

In the days before he died, Elmer spoke with the older boys individually, asking them if they regretted joining him in this struggling business. They all told him no.

Bob remembered telling his father, "With all we have been through and experienced, we have learned so much that nothing could stop us."

John recalled Elmer saying to him, "Listen. This is going to pay off. You'll have your day," and Elmer assured Gina, "These boys know how to run the business. Don't worry about them."

And Gina didn't worry. Gina never worried. Her faith was so strong she always believed that things would end up working out for the best. Her children, however, were deeply concerned.

The reality was the business was buried by an avalanche of debt, and the restaurants were not yet profit-making ventures. Despite small successes like Ginel, which at the time was the linchpin of the business, the prognosis was grim.

At the time of Elmer's death, Bob was the de facto head of the enterprise. He pulled the numbers together to indicate exactly what shape the company was in: about $1 million in trade debt, business and personal liens placed on them by the Internal Revenue Service because the company was behind on its taxes, a top line that was growing too slowly, and a bottom line that was unsustainable.

But none of it mattered. Over a series of family meetings, as the children took stock of the company and of themselves, they realized they had no choice. To quit now would be to subject themselves—and their mother—to financial ruin. The harsh truth was their only option was to push on and try to turn the business around.

"Our thinking was day-to-day," recalled John, "how to survive. How to pay the bills. I remember walking with my wife [Carolyn], thinking we couldn't wait until we finished paying off the note for the Bon-Bon. At the time, we thought that was the biggest hurdle to face, and if we could just get to that point, everything would be okay."

Years later, Doug would compare the situation to "being in a leaky lifeboat in the middle of the ocean. If you jump out, you die. You have to continue to bail and patch the boat as best you can and try to make it to shore."

Looking back, Mike could see the faith their father had in this family endeavor—enough to work through these challenges. "My dad always felt that all his children had strengths and talents. He tried to outline the company when he was alive and set it up so we would gravitate to our natural areas of experience. He always saw this bigger picture before we ever did."

"Pop knew how to make the right decisions, but he let us make the wrong ones so we could learn from our mistakes," shared John. "It's what helped us to overcome so many obstacles along the way. He was courageous in starting this business, putting every nickel and dime he had on the line. When he was supposed to be enjoying his latter years, he was building our foundation. We weren't about to let that fail."

What they didn't yet realize was that the seeds of growth and success had already begun to germinate. They had been sown three years earlier by Charlie Chiesa, the human resources director for Travelers Insurance, whose offices were on 7th Street in Garden City, about two blocks away from the Bon-Bon.

Chiesa was a regular breakfast customer at the Bon-Bon, even though Travelers had a cafeteria for its 500 employees. But Chiesa preferred the food and the atmosphere at the coffee shop. Plus, he liked Elmer. He enjoyed talking with him, and he sensed in Elmer that desire to do whatever it took to satisfy customers. So, one day, he asked Elmer if the family would be interested in taking over his company's foodservice operation.

As with the restaurant, the family knew nothing about managing a corporate dining facility. However, they liked the fact that, for the first time in their business's young life, they would not be assuming much risk. Chiesa assured them there would be no rent or other overhead expenses to cover. There would be no weekends to work, just breakfast and lunch business five days a week.

So Elmer put together a business proposal and presented it to Chiesa's bosses. Travelers accepted the bid, and in 1981, the Whitcombs entered the contract foodservice management business.

As they would later do for Ginel, the Whitcombs built most of what they needed in their garage over the course of two weekends. What they couldn't make, they bought at what Doug called "the chip and dent store."

The contract was immediately successful, generating $500 a day in sales. In the beginning, the crew prepared food at the Bon-Bon and transported it to Travelers. Eventually, they shifted gears, making some items such as soups and sauces at the restaurant and preparing sandwiches and other foods on-site.

Over the next few years, the contract management business would slowly take shape, and the Whitcombs would try their hand at various industry segments. In 1982, they landed an account for Hazeltine Corp., a defense contractor.

Headquartered in Greenlawn, Hazeltine had four locations on Long Island with cafeterias and another ten that offered vending only. The client wanted Whitsons to handle both the manual and vending services. So, the Whitcombs created a vending business out of a storeroom at Hazeltine. They bought some reconditioned machines and hired someone to stock the machines on a regular basis. Later, they would hire mechanics to service the machines.

Over time, this subset of the business grew, with Whitsons adding vending to many of its accounts. Soon, the company had hundreds of machines. But, Bob remembered, it became a distraction to Whitsons' core business. It was not a direction the Whitcombs were interested in moving.

So, in 1987, they sold the vending business. The new owners added Whitsons' vending employees to their payroll, and Whitsons became the company's first account. Ultimately, however, the new owners were unable to make the business work, and Whitsons ended up taking the vending back.

From then on, they operated vending in a mixed fashion, managing it for some accounts and contracting it out for others. Finally, in 2013, the Whitcombs sold the vending division to Answer Vending.

Growing the contract management business was a laborious process. Whitsons was like an expansion team in a pro sports league. There were plenty of established players in the market, a few of them national in scope. Going head-to-head against even the smaller regional companies was a daunting task for Whitsons because the company had no track record. It was an unknown entity.

In the eyes of the largest potential clients, Whitsons simply wasn't qualified to run their cafeterias. So, the company had no other choice but to seek out accounts that either were too small for the bigger contractors to be interested in or too much trouble for them to be bothered with.

That's where the boys' wrestling background came in handy: go for the smaller wins to build the strength and capacity for larger ones later. This had become a winning strategy for the solutions-focused family with a legacy to preserve.

There were clients such as Nassau County Community College, an institution that had grown faster than its foodservice could keep up with. As a result, dining facilities were old and in desperate need of repair. There was also the Mineola Court Complex, a collection of Nassau County buildings that included the County Office Building, the Criminal Court Building, and the Social Services Office.

Public colleges and government offices can be notoriously difficult to deal with because tight budgets and/or the politically charged atmosphere of these institutions make it tough to satisfy customers, please clients, *and* turn a profit. And when Whitsons secured one of these contracts, it would have to outperform its client's expectations. Each account had to become an unqualified recommendation for the next potential piece of business.

The problem was that Whitsons' accounts were not showplaces where you would walk in and marvel at the design, and the Whitcombs had no extra cash to make more than essential cosmetic or equipment changes.

So, the company had no choice but to sell itself on the quality of its food and the warmth of its customer service. In addition, the company's retention rate had to be virtually 100% in order for Whitsons to demonstrate its ability to operate any type of account.

"We knew we were different from other companies, but not quite sure how to articulate that in a business heavily focused on financial return," explained John. "Quality is not cheap, but we were not willing to sacrifice the integrity of our upbringing for an extra dime. It was a challenge to find the right formula for us; what market(s) could we work with that valued what we had to offer? How could we make cost-effective improvements at the same time? Who were the right partners for us?"

Over the next several years, Whitsons dabbled in nearly every business segment: corporate dining; college dining; residential units such as homeless shelters, halfway houses, and homes for juvenile offenders; healthcare foodservice; school foodservice; vending; and off-premise catering as the Whitcombs sought to find their niche in the world of contract management.

One unfortunate commonality between the restaurants and contract accounts—particularly in the business and industry ("B&I") dining segment—was that there always seemed to be employees who wanted to play the system for their own benefit.

"When we branched out into corporate dining, we seemed to be doing well, but we still were not yielding the profits we had hoped for," Bob recalled. "Our trusting nature and our lack of a decent system for financial paperwork led some managers to be able to skim money off the top by doctoring the books."

Bob said that when he realized that Whitsons was likely again being taken advantage of, he decided to employ a "secret weapon": his wife, MaryLou, Doug's wife, Diane, and John's wife, Carolyn. The three women began making spot checks of B&I accounts, showing up unannounced to pull out register drawers and perform cash-outs.

As word spread of these surprise visits, Whitsons began finding fewer discrepancies in the books. The company also began to enhance its financial system as better record-keeping programs emerged on the market, and profitability increased.

"Our father founded this business on transparency and integrity, and while those we tried to do business with didn't always share that philosophy, we were determined to keep it that way, for ourselves and for our customers," Doug revealed. And it's a company value that holds true to this day.

Through it all, Whitsons continued to make headway in the industry by gathering up unwanted accounts and, sometimes, by catching the competition off guard. For example, in 1985, when Long Island Lighting opened a new office just outside Garden City, Bob discovered that the building was not covered by the foodservice contract LILCO had negotiated for its other offices.

So, the Whitcombs offered to provide food for this one location. Five years later, when the contract for all of LILCO's locations went out to bid, Whitsons was able to secure the entire business.

While the contract management side of the business was in its infancy, Bob, Doug, and John once again took the lead. The family voted that Bob should be in charge of the company, and Doug stepped into the role of the chief salesman while John led operations.

It would work out well; Bob seemed to have a head for administration while, as his brother John explained it, "Doug never saw a piece of business he didn't think had potential."

The Whitcombs managed operations out of the basement of the Bon-Bon. To reach the two-room "headquarters," you either walked into the kitchen, past the dish room, and down a narrow staircase, or you entered from the outside by walking down an alley crowded with garbage from the restaurant and adjacent businesses. The office space was home primarily to two bookkeepers, who kept track of the business with paper ledgers, register tapes, and the like.

They spent their days tallying numbers to the constant whine of compressors and the plunking of the ice machine, which dropped a fresh batch of ice cubes every eight minutes. The setting wouldn't exactly incite confidence in Whitsons in the eyes of prospective business partners. So, vendors and potential clients were always entertained upstairs in the Bon-Bon's dining room.

When one of the Whitcombs was in the "office" speaking on the phone with a customer, he would explain away the noise as the inevitable construction associated with a growing company.

Despite this makeshift setup, Whitsons slowly continued to build its non-restaurant business. One notable account was the Kaufman Astoria Studios in Queens. The company managed the commissary for this location, which was the original headquarters of Paramount Pictures in the 1920s and continued to be a prime location for shooting movies and TV series.

But the account became noteworthy for Whitsons not because the Whitcombs were rubbing elbows with actors, directors, and producers but because of the role it would play in helping to establish what today is a major driver for the company's growth: the prepared meals division.

In the spring of 1987, Bob received a phone call from the manager of the Borden Avenue Veterans Residence in Long Island City. As the name suggested, Borden Avenue was a homeless shelter for military veterans operated by the Salvation Army.

The manager had heard of Whitsons' reputation for serving high-quality food, and he wanted to know whether the company would be willing to cater a luncheon at the shelter. It was to be a large affair with nearly 400 people in attendance, including New York City Mayor Ed Koch. Bob didn't hesitate to say yes. He wrote down all the details and promised the Army "a magnificent show."

There was the usual back-and-forth between the company and the client as a menu was written and approved, pricing was agreed upon, and foodstuffs were purchased. Everything was perfect, save for one tiny detail: during his original call with the manager, Bob had written down the wrong date, a day later than the event was actually scheduled.

On the day of the event, a couple of hours before the luncheon was to begin, staff at the Bon-Bon were busily preparing food they assumed was going to be served the next day when Bob received a phone call from an understandably worried Joe Cheney, house manager at Borden Avenue, asking him where the food was. Bob was, to use his word, "mortified" by his mistake.

Whitsons had never left a customer in the lurch, and its chief executive wasn't about to set a new precedent. He alerted his team, and everyone began scrambling to pull together what they could. Bob even enlisted the help of a business broker, who happened to be at the Bon-Bon hoping to be engaged to sell the restaurant when the call came in. The broker was sent to the bakery down the street to pick up the petits fours that the bakery had prepared for the event.

Years later, Bob still couldn't fathom exactly how the team managed to pull it off, but they arrived on-site with everything they needed with only minutes to spare, and the event was a great success. The Army was so amazed at the quality of the meal that not only was the house manager willing to forgive Bob his faux pas, but the Salvation Army's Director of Homeless Services, Alfred Peck, wanted to hire Whitsons to provide foodservice for the shelter on a daily basis.

However, because the shelter's kitchen wasn't large enough to prepare all the meals that were needed, Whitsons agreed to prepare and plate the meals off-site and deliver them to Borden Avenue to be reheated and served.

Because of Astoria's proximity to Long Island City, the Kaufman Astoria Studios' kitchen became Whitsons' first production center, specifically for meals at the Borden Avenue shelter.

That's when then-new team member Chris Fautas showed his versatility as a valuable member of the team, able to take on a multitude of roles as needed. Formerly employed by Service America Corp., Fautas had met Bob at several industry networking functions in the 1980s. He admired Bob, and he liked the thought of working for a smaller family business. At Service America, at the time one of the largest foodservice contractors in the U.S., Fautas felt that he was just a number. At a company such as Whitsons, he thought, individuals could have a bigger chance to help mold the direction of the company.

Fautas interviewed for a district manager's slot in 1992, and although he wasn't offered the position, the Whitcombs liked him enough to make him a unit manager at Morgan Postal Service in New York City. After about 18 months, he was moved to Kaufman Astoria Studios, and a year and a half after that, he became a district manager. Now serving as vice president of compliance and project management, Fautas' 31-year tenure with Whitsons holds memories that go far back as he recalled his initiation into the prepared meals world at Kaufman.

"During the day, we ran the commissary for the studio. Then, the team would come at night and prepare the meals for the Salvation Army and the city, and our two drivers would deliver the meals in vans. They'd finish up at 4 in the morning, and by 5 o'clock, we were rolling back to commissary duties. It was a 24-hour operation."

Emmitt Davis, a 33-year Whitsons veteran who still works at the company today at the Brooklyn Culinary Center, was one of those original two drivers.

"I started out at Kaufman serving the Salvation Army's Borden Avenue center," Davis recounted. "I really enjoyed delivering meals to the people there—they liked the meals and were grateful for them every day. We'd deliver meals in a van with our name on it, which made us feel special. That van kept our food safe, and we never missed a delivery, but we quickly learned that we couldn't drive it too fast because it would smoke like a freight train.

"I remember my boss joking, 'You ain't driving no Cadillac, Emmitt, but it'll get you where you are going.' And it did, and I did the best job that I could to make people happy. I was glad when we retired that vehicle and got new vans, though. We've really come a long way since those days."

"There were so many great people like Emmitt who supported the beginnings of this division," said Fautas. "Another memorable team member, Khalid Efat, was actually a physician during the week but would continue to come in to run the operation on weekends. I'd literally ask him why he would do that, and he'd say, 'I just want to give back to the community. It's not about the money.' He stayed on with us for years, helping us to open our Queens center. We had no shortage of extraordinary individuals like this over the years."

Demand for prepared meals grew as word spread, and over the next few years, Whitsons moved production from one account to another as the need for more kitchen space grew. Eventually, a hub and spoke system was set up, with meals being prepared at the US Post Office in Melville, a Whitsons account that at the time had the largest kitchen available. But it didn't take long for the demand to outgrow even that kitchen's capacity. Eventually, a center in Queens was set up to help run this part of the business, closely followed by Whitsons' first official corporate production center in Huntington Station.

***

As the Whitcombs worked to make inroads into contract management and work out its prepared meals component, they still had the restaurants to contend with. It seemed inevitable that both the Bon-Bon and Blue Chip would fail.

No matter what moves the family made, they could not grow business in these coffee shops. The Bon-Bon's lunch business was at capacity, but despite the marketing or advertising that was done, business at breakfast and dinner never grew. The Blue Chip, open from 6 am to 3:30 pm, was a break-even business at best, certainly not enough to make up for any losses at the Bon-Bon.

Finally, in 1986, the Whitcombs paid off the loan on the Blue Chip.

But there was little time, or cause, for celebration. The building's owner—the Whitcombs had bought the restaurants, but not the buildings in which they were situated—decided he would prefer to lease the space to something more attractive, such as an upscale clothing store. He told the Whitcombs that if they wanted to renew their lease, the rent was going to be triple what it had been. The Whitcombs chose not to renew the lease and allowed the Blue Chip to die quietly.

They would not be as lucky with the Bon-Bon. As 1987 rolled on, traffic along Franklin Avenue continued to decline, with more and more shoppers heading to Roosevelt Field Mall. So, not only could the Whitcombs not increase customer counts, but they were starting to lose what steady diners they had.

In addition, they realized that if they planned to hold on to the restaurant, they would have to invest in some repairs and upgrades. The family decided it wasn't worth it. The Whitcombs now could see the direction the company was headed, and the Bon-Bon did not fit their vision.

It was time to give up the ghost, as it were. So, in 1988, the Whitcombs sold the Bon-Bon for a fraction of the original purchase price and were happy to do so. They rented a space on West Hills Road in Huntington, 1,500 square feet of what used to be an auto repair shop, for a new office and concentrated on seeking out new foodservice accounts to manage.

"One of the most promising moments is when we moved our business to this building," Bob recalls. "In the midst of all this turmoil [with the restaurants], we found an opportunity to keep moving ourselves forward. It symbolized hope."

By the end of the 1980s, they would have more than $7 million in top-line business from such companies as Esselte Pendaflex, Hazeltine, Designatronics, and Kaufman Astoria Studios. During that time, Whitsons also secured its first residential services account, Lincoln Hall Boys' Home in Westchester County, NY, and its first school account, Hicksville School District on Long Island.

But the Bon-Bon still had one more opportunity to cause grief for the young company's owners—again, due to the trusting and generous nature of the family. In negotiating the sale, instead of demanding monthly repayment of the loan, the Whitcombs gave the new owners a balloon note for the first year.

This, theoretically, would give the owners time to get themselves settled and try to grow the business. But when Bob went to collect the note one year later, the owners refused to pay. Bob discovered that they had "managed to run the business into the ground."

The owners were behind on their rent, and they owed vendors as well as the Whitcombs. So, the Whitcombs decided to void the sale and reclaim the Bon-Bon. But when Bob arrived at the restaurant with all the proper documentation in hand to seize the business, the owners refused to let him in the building.

Bob called the police, but the 15 minutes it took for authorities to arrive was all the owners needed. They broke dishes and equipment, slashed the booths with knives, and punctured holes in the compressors with an ice pick. The Bon-Bon was a total loss.

"It was absolutely heartbreaking," Bob remembered. "This was the place where my father started it all. To see it fall in this way was something we all took very personally. It was more than just a business to us."

Still, in retrospect, the Whitcombs understood that the restaurant had been a valuable learning experience. It helped teach them the ins and outs of the foodservice industry.

Through their dealings with diners and vendors, they have come in contact with a number of people willing to reward Whitcombs' work ethic and customer service approach with financial help and business leads. Their faith continued to surprise them in the most unexpected ways.

The experience also taught them the hard way about the need to manage food and labor costs. Bob said, "We now knew how to become profitable." The company had manual systems in place to hold employees accountable. Computer systems were beginning to be used to track accounting and financial data. They paid attention to the smallest details that would add up to their success.

The Whitcombs were a formidable bunch; there was no way they were backing down.

Amazingly, the struggling family business not only survived the decade but also achieved a modicum of success without ever stiffing a vendor or the government and without once declaring bankruptcy. Not many companies can claim that same virtuosity—or resilience.

"When everyone else would have walked away, we were either too stubborn or too stupid to quit," admitted Doug. "Some of it has been magical, and some of it miraculous. But most of it is blood, sweat, and tears—and the payoff was our ability to succeed when no one else thought it was possible."

The "leaky lifeboat" had finally made it to shore, and the next decade would see slow but steady and continual growth.

5.
More Growing Pains

The 1990s were a series of beginnings for Whitsons as the company began stretching its legs and experimenting with new lines of business. By the time the new millennium dawned, some of those sources of income would become firmly established, while others either would be fading or already written off as the family found they did not fit the company's business model.

The process would also spark more than a few disagreements among the family members as the siblings debated the wisdom of almost every move to be made.

"There was almost always pressure," Bob recalled. "We had just gotten out from under the restaurants, and we were growing, but we weren't so secure that we didn't worry about everything we were doing.

"We'd have debates, and sometimes people weren't always at their best, but the great thing about our family is that we didn't hold grudges. Fifteen minutes after an argument, it was over. There was never any lasting damage to our relationships."

"Things could get heated," John agreed. "People would feel very passionate about their respective positions. But we understood it was business. It wasn't personal. We said our piece, and then the family made a decision and moved on."

And so, Whitsons' corporate tree slowly grew and branched, beginning in 1989 when the company signed its first school account, the Hicksville School District. Hicksville, best known as the hometown of singer/songwriter Billy Joel, is a hamlet of about 42,000 people within Oyster Bay, Long Island.

The district comprises seven elementary schools, a middle school, and a high school. John, who would manage the school foodservice business in its early years, noted that the family took on the Hicksville district using the same approach that had worked so well in Whitsons' corporate accounts; that is, prepare great food, give the students a wide variety of items, and sell them à la carte.

But John quickly learned that, just as in the restaurant business, there was a lot to understand about managing school cafeterias, and not all of the lessons learned in restaurants would be transferable to schools. It would take him the better part of a decade to get a handle on it all.

"When people think about school foodservice, they think: 'How difficult can that be?' But it's incredibly challenging," he says.

"The conditions are challenging and fast-paced, and you have to answer to everybody: employees, students, parents, school district administrators, and state and federal regulators. There are so many things you have to juggle, and no two days are alike. You are constantly running, and you do everything: marketing, PR, purchasing, nutrition, menu planning, and training."

One of those conditions that John had to absorb was that in school districts that are part of the National School Lunch Program (NSLP), administered by the US Department of Agriculture, à la carte sales are discouraged.

As John and his brothers soon discovered, "It's a heavily regulated industry that comes with its own compliance requirements that involved a steep learning curve."

Because the stated goal of the program is to provide nutritious meals for children, the USDA reimburses districts on the basis of the number of meals served that meet the USDA's nutritional guidelines. Whitsons had the process backward, pushing à la carte sales at the expense of the reimbursable meals, and as a result, lost money in its first year of operation in Hicksville.

John and his team would have to learn the ins and outs of free and reduced-price meals, the purchase and use of USDA commodities, the ever-changing nutrition standards regulating the amount of salt, fat, and sugar in kids' meals, and the nuances of the state bid process for different government entities.

The challenges would be compounded as the company expanded its education business into Connecticut and Massachusetts and, eventually, New Jersey and Pennsylvania. They would discover that laws and processes were sometimes different from one state to another. In short, great food and service—the hallmark of Whitsons from day one—were not always the first criteria in the selection process.

"It was yet another learning curve we had to endure as we explored new territories," explained John. "The most obvious was the financial, legal, and bidding differences, where no two states were alike in their approach. But then there was the constant struggle to make a name for ourselves in an unknown area: in order to qualify to bid, you had to have a certain number of years of experience specifically in that state—and yet, how could we get that experience if no doors were opening?"

Paul also remembers how hard the company fought against that limiting criterion to be included in the process for fair competition. In the end, they found their way in, again, with their magical formula: finding smaller districts that were looking for something other than the large corporations and willing to waive that requirement to give the unknown Whitsons a chance.

"That's when our name was starting to mean something in the industry. We discovered how appealing it was to be a more hands-on, family company in a world of conglomerates—yet with all the resources they needed for a successful program," said Paul, who by this time was working with Doug to steadily build strategic growth plans and growing the organization's sales team.

These resources have evolved over the years, but having Hicksville as its first school client benefited Whitsons in more ways than one. First, Hicksville was a district starving for a new foodservice program. The district managed its own foodservice at two middle schools and the high school, but none of the seven elementary schools had offered school lunches for several years.

So, Whitsons had the opportunity to start fresh and implement the kind of program that the students would respond to. The company hired the foodservice staff that had been on the district's payroll and added a few dozen additional staff to help reopen the elementary schools. The first few months were rough because parents had to be made aware of the fact that the elementary schools were again offering lunch.

John said the middle and high school students responded well—and quickly—to the expanded menu variety and food quality that Whitsons offered. But the elementary program was slower to take off, and it was nearly Christmas of 1989 before Whitsons began to see serious gains in elementary school participation.

The company also had to learn the fine art of predicting the percentages of free, reduced-price, and full-paid meals it would serve in the account, as well as what income it could generate in à la carte sales. The reimbursement matrix works best when all three categories of meals are maximized.

As for à la carte sales, John said, "You had to nail it. If you predicted X dollars a day, you had better hit that."

The other benefit that accrued from dealing with a New York school district first was that Whitsons was able to forge a fiscally strong operating model. New York is one of a few states that have a bidding process that focuses exclusively on fixed-meal costs. Most other states feature some form of cost-reimbursable or best value calculations in their bid proposals. So, John and his team learned how to combine a restaurant mentality for quality with a school mentality for low cost. They learned from the Hicksville experience and then applied that knowledge to bids for other Long Island districts.

Then, as they adapted, they were able to expand off Long Island and into Westchester County, winning some significant contracts such as the Mount Vernon School District, which encompasses more than 8,000 students in 11 elementary schools, two middle schools, and three high schools.

Then, when they moved into Connecticut and Massachusetts, they discovered that the financial skills learned by negotiating the New York state bid process gave them the upper hand in competing for contracts in those states.

Despite the fact that Whitsons lost money initially at Hicksville, the team's customer service skills and its strong desire to succeed eventually made it profitable there, and Hicksville remains a client to this day. But the company would hit many bumps in the road as it forged ahead.

Their brother Mike, who managed school districts for a while in the 1990s, said the company "didn't fully comprehend the state and federal guidelines, and until we learned these, we continued to make mistakes."

Sometimes, the Whitcombs' faith protected them in unusual ways. Mike recalled an incident where a woman from the local health department was inspecting the district's kitchens. While Mike was in her eyesight, he committed a minor infraction. He sampled a piece of sliced meat without wearing a glove.

When the inspector approached him to write him up, however, she noticed that he was wearing a "rosary ring," a ring with a small cross at the top and ten bumps around the ring to represent one decade of the rosary. Some Catholics use it to pray when pulling out a standard rosary isn't possible.

"She said to me, 'Because you're wearing that,'" Mike recalled. "'I'm going to let you go on this. But do you realize what you just did?'" Mike silently thanked God and made a mental note never to do it again.

In ways like this, just as they had in the restaurants, the Whitcombs learned from their errors. They slowly began to grasp the nuances and vagaries of the elementary and secondary school environment, and success followed. When Whitsons came up with its next big innovation in 1994, the Whitcombs set themselves up for greater success not only in schools but in B&I and other segments as well.

That idea was the Signature Series branded concepts program, which was developed by John and a young executive by the name of Kelly Friend. Friend had been hired at about the same time Whitsons was becoming involved with school foodservice. She had been working at a restaurant in Manhattan, but she was getting married and wanted to move to Long Island.

Friend responded to an ad Whitsons had placed for a B&I general manager and met one day in the summer of 1989 with Doug at the account where the manager's position needed to be filled.

"We hit it off immediately," Friend recalled. "The Whitcombs had incredible instincts, and they were all entrepreneurs at heart whether they realized it or not. They ran their business by treating people the way they themselves wanted to be treated, and it was different from anything I had experienced before."

At the end of the interview, Doug handed Friend the keys to the account and said, "Be here tomorrow at 7 am." She worked as a unit manager for a while and then joined Doug on the road as a salesperson, focusing on the K-12 market. But she was also tasked with doing some marketing as well. So when it came time for John to make his dream of a branded program a reality, he turned to Friend. The two of them led a team that would create the framework for the Signature Series.

"We were already bringing the restaurant mentality to our accounts," said John. "I decided that we could create our own brands to mimic the QSRs at a minimal cost. Then, they could easily be swapped out as customers got bored with a concept or were clamoring for a different type of cuisine."

The first concept created was the Great American Sandwich Company. At this station, customers could have their sandwiches made to order by selecting from a line of premium cold cuts, cheeses, protein salads, or vegetables on their choice of bread. Or, they could choose from a menu of prepared sandwiches that could be grilled in a panini press or toasted in a conveyor oven.

Five other concepts quickly followed in that first wave. As the market evolved, so too did the Signature Series, adding, revising, and removing concepts in line with the current trends and customer demands.

With over 25 developed concepts over the years, some of the most popular have included La Cucina, an Italian concept; Miss Ruby's Grill, a traditional grill station; Elmer's Famous Foods, a rotisserie concept; Coyote Grill, a Tex-Mex outlet; and The Veggie Table, an array of vegetarian entrées, developed by Whitsons with the help of vegetarian chef Claire Criscuolo, owner of Claire's Corner Copia in New Haven, CT.

Some of the concepts, such as Miss Ruby's Grill, have several variations, so some versions of the concept can be fitted to virtually any type of account. Also, many of these programs have sub-sets with specific menus.

Today, the company continues to expand its menu innovation with an award-winning concept, Pop-Up Shops, which takes the premise of these branded stations and features them as day-long promotions to spice up the offerings. (This idea was such an immediate success that the Whitsons Pop-Up Shops promotion was recognized in 2022 by *Food Management,* an industry trade magazine, with its Best Concept Award.)

***

The 1990s brought more firsts for Whitsons. One was the first account in the state of New Jersey: Tommy Hilfiger, in Dayton. A second and more significant achievement was the company's first full-fledged college account, the New York Institute of Technology, with campuses in Central Islip and Westbury on Long Island.

Although Whitsons had managed foodservice for Nassau Community College in the 1980s, NYIT was the first college account that featured both residential and retail dining programs.

At first, colleges seemed to be a natural fit for Whitsons because they closely resembled B&I operations—at least on the retail side. But as the family was soon to learn, there were challenges inherent both in working a college account and trying to grow the college business. With regard to operating a specific account, there were two problems, and neither one involved students.

"Pleasing the students was not the hard part," John said. "Pleasing the customer is never the hard part. The challenge was getting through all of the layers that were between us and the customers."

Indeed, dealing with bureaucratic administrators historically has been a headache for most contract management companies. It begins with the bidding process. Most university administrators, particularly those at large universities, look for two things from a company when putting a contract out for bid: to feed students for the lowest possible cost and to be willing to invest their own funds upfront to renovate dining facilities. The largest contractors are often prepared to do that, sometimes handing over tens of millions of dollars while structuring their bids so that they are better able to recoup their investment over the life of the contract.

Then, once a contractor is on-site, it has to deal with the changing political climate of the institution. It is not uncommon for a contractor to be replaced simply because an incoming president or a trustee with clout prefers another company. Beyond that, there are the ups and downs of the market cycle to deal with.

When school is in session, business is good. However, with semesters starting and stopping and the inevitable summer hiatus, it is often difficult for contractors to plan their businesses. Although K-12 schools also have that summer break, the business during the school year is more predictable and, therefore, easier to manage.

So, although Whitsons was able to win as many as eight university accounts in the mid-to late-1990s, the Whitcombs ultimately decided that this market didn't fit with the company's growth strategy. So, as contracts ran out, Whitsons simply declined to rebid. By the early 2000s, the company was out of the higher education business.

The decade also saw the launch of Whitsons' catering division.

The division grew out of the company's involvement with its first "specialty" account: the Unqua Yacht Club in Amityville, NY. The club, where Whitsons managed foodservice for two years in the early '90s, was almost 180 degrees from any of the company's other accounts. Whereas other businesses consisted of breakfasts and lunches Monday through Friday, the yacht club business consisted of lunches and dinners seven days a week.

Young Andy cut his eyeteeth at Whitsons in this account, and it was here, he said, that he became "truly enchanted with preparing high-end food." Although the yacht club would return to self-operation with the arrival of a new commodore, the Whitcombs had learned about the possibilities of upscale foodservice and so decided to create their own gourmet catering business called Whitsons Fabulous Foods.

The name didn't stick; the Whitcombs discovered there was already a catering company in the tri-state area called Fabulous

Foods, so they eventually renamed the division Andrews. For 14 years, Whitsons made a name for itself on Long Island as a high-quality and reasonably priced off-premise caterer. It was a nice added service for clients who wanted to make use of it, and it was a good source of revenue from events such as weddings, christenings, and bar mitzvahs. It also gave way to unique opportunities, such as managing the New York Jets' temporary foodservice and involvement in the design and construction of their new training facility cafe.

Doug's son, Craig Whitcomb, and Bill's son, Bill Whitcomb, Jr., got their start working for Andrews. Both recalled the work as both challenging and exhilarating, never able to say "no" to any request.

"We catered everywhere. It didn't matter," said Bill. "We would do weddings outside on beaches, dragging ovens and hot boxes through sand in order to make a client's day special."

"We'd even execute an event under the most difficult of environments—one being a 350-person plated sit-down dinner in a polo field for a high-profile celebrity," Craig added. "For us, it was a nightmare. There were no facilities. We had to bring in a mobile kitchen to cook the food there on-site, present it, and then serve it."

There was also the ongoing service on the Lauren Kristy Paddleboat, where the catering team was confined to a makeshift kitchen down below in the boat with no windows or air—in the middle of the summer.

One of Craig's favorite examples of pulling off the impossible was a wedding cake snafu turned genius. The bride and groom had ordered a custom Napoleon-style cake for the celebration, but before the team arrived on-site, a crate of ice fell right into it, creating a gaping hole in its center.

Thinking quickly on their feet, the team stopped by a grocery store to pick up canned whipped cream and fresh flowers to fill in the hole. By the time they were done, they had transformed the cake's center into an aesthetic masterpiece that the guests raved about.

Craig laughed as he told the story. "To this day, I still cannot believe the elated note of thanks from the bride telling us it was the most beautiful cake they'd ever seen. But it reminded us that we had what it took to make every event special, no matter what went right or wrong. We made it a point to always say 'yes,' figure out the details later, and then execute it."

And that reputation for service led to the opportunity to cater meals for the New York Jets. As the training grounds for the national sports team, Hofstra University was in search of a caterer to provide five meals a day (breakfast, lunch, dinner, and two hot snacks), six days a week, to a group of 175 team members. When Whitsons got the call, they were ready to take on the challenge. Little did they know the complexity of service it would require.

The only way to deliver this program was to bring in a food truck and set it up in the parking lot—a deluxe mobile kitchen known as the "Silver Bullet." It was a unique experience unlike they've ever known, as they didn't have the on-site tools or operations resources they were used to having as a contract management or off-premises caterer.

"I practically lived in that Silver Bullet for two years," Craig said. "But what we learned was invaluable: execution through adversity. We had to learn to be nimble and prepare meals 'just in time.' We had to adjust our ordering process and get creative with our storage practices. It took what we knew about catering and pushed us beyond our limits—in a good way."

Taking on that challenge ultimately led to Whitsons' being brought in by the Jets to assist them with the construction of their new on-site café in New Jersey. From design and equipment suggestions to construction walkthroughs and a grand opening, Whitsons was proud to help build a first-class dining establishment reminiscent of a corporate café to serve the players, coaches, and back office staff. While this partnership only lasted a few years, it remains one of the most rewarding educational experiences for the Andrews catering division.

Through the years, the company partnered with different locations to provide high-end event packages, including Coindre Hall, the Vanderbilt Mansion, and Oheka Castle, not to mention various vineyards, golf courses, and nightclubs.

Ultimately, however, the Whitcombs decided that off-premise

catering was not the future of the company. They found it to be a very seasonal business and it required physical assets and space that were different from those on the contract management side.

"What ended up happening," Paul explained, "was that we worked really hard generating revenue from spring until fall—prime wedding season—and lost money over the winter. In the end, it wasn't profitable enough to be part of our long-term plan."

What the Whitcombs were learning was that each market they entered, each line of business with which they became involved, was specialized. Each had its own opportunities and its unique challenges. Also, it wasn't easy to find management employees who could operate in more than one segment. So, the company would either have to hire a lot more people or decide which segments made the most sense to focus on.

The Whitcombs chose the latter, and for them, it would turn out to be the right choice.

One of the biggest changes for Whitsons came in 1996 when the company bought an 11,000-square-foot building on Oakwood Road in Huntington. It was notable for a couple of reasons. First, it was the first corporate headquarters that the Whitcombs actually owned.

From the Bon-Bon to the converted auto repair shop on West Hills Road in Huntington, Whitsons had always occupied leased space. So, Oakwood Road became a huge source of pride for the family. It signaled just how far the company had come since the days of debating which bill to pay first with the meager income available.

"One of the most exciting things to happen to us was when they built this building," recalled Gina. "I saw the company grow from a small office in the basement under the Bon-Bon to a lovely building where there were accommodations for everybody. It was a big thrill for me to see it grow—it's more than I could have ever asked for."

The building would also house the company's first bona fide production center. More than seven times larger than the previous office space, the building's size was a real necessity for the growing enterprise. Through word of mouth, the prepared meals business had blossomed. What had started out as a reward from the Salvation Army for pulling off a catering miracle had become a nearly $2 million business. The Post Office kitchen in Melville could no longer accommodate the number of meals that were needed to keep up with demand.

So, the Whitcombs decided to devote 5,000 square feet of the new building to a production center for prepared meals.

"When we started, we had to transition from a catering company to a very sophisticated production operation with a hub and spoke system with everything made centrally," Bob explained. "It was new but very exciting."

Exciting—but with a dash more lessons to come. While there were similarities in standards between contract management and prepared meal guidelines, the team quickly learned that there were critical intricacies between child nutrition and senior feeding.

In fact, Mike, who found a passion for working in this aspect of the business, was so moved by the prevalence of malnutrition among the senior community that he began focusing business efforts on bridging the gap in this market.

"Too many homebound seniors were not getting access to the meals and nutrients they required just to stay healthy," he explained. "It became our mission to source and support as many senior programs as possible within our reach to do our part to help those who needed it most."

But the commitment to being community-minded did not stop there. It became a tradition for team members to volunteer their time to provide hot, fresh meals for the homeless at Thanksgiving through the Salvation Army. Volunteers would come in and prepare the food—including whole turkeys—early in the morning and sometimes work the night before in order to deliver hot meals to over 3,000 thankful individuals each year.

Through delivered meal services, the Whitcombs found they had the best of both worlds: creating business opportunities and providing service to others.

With the restaurant business behind them and a bright future in contract management and prepared meals ahead, the Whitcomb family was optimistic about the years to come and proud of all they had accomplished to turn their challenges around. The new headquarters symbolized their resilience and hope for the future.

At the suggestion of Bob's wife, MaryLou, the family dedicated the building to Elmer, and a bronze plaque for the lobby was created. The plaque reads:

> *"A man whose gentle nature, unselfishness, and love of family started us on the road to success and ultimately led us to where we are today. This building is a reminder to all of us that you are watching from above and will continue to guide us in the right direction. Thanks, Pop."*

A version of this plaque now hangs in all of Whitsons' Culinary Centers.

Moving into the new headquarters at Oakwood, family members and team members alike thought they were in foodservice heaven. They believed that they would never outgrow the space.

They were wrong. Within two years, as Doug explained, "Business had quadrupled, and you couldn't fit a toothpick in that kitchen."

With the new millennium approaching, Whitsons was no longer that "leaky lifeboat" that struggled to stay afloat in a sea of financial troubles. It was now a sleek sailing ship, with its course becoming more defined as time flowed on.

6.
The Family Expands

Through all the growing pains, one thing remained constant: the desire to remain a family. But not just a family of nine siblings—a family of people committed to working together to make the world a better place.

This became evident throughout the 1990s as the Whitcombs recognized how many employees remained by their side from the earlier years. Whitsons' team members were loyal because they felt like they were part of the family from the very beginning. It was never an intended strategy for the Whitcombs; it was just their natural way of being that created an environment where people mattered.

Friend knew this was the place for her from the moment she met the family.

"One of my fondest memories of working with Whitsons happened while sitting in a sales meeting. A prospective client, who eventually became a long-term client, inadvertently referred to me as 'Kelly Whitcomb,' assuming that because there were three other Whitcombs in attendance, I was also a family member. When I started to correct her and provide my actual surname, Doug stopped me right there and said, 'Kelly may have another legal name, but she will always be a Whitcomb to us. She is definitely a family member.'"

Now retired, Renee Calderon is known as one of the longest-standing team members, working for Whitsons for 44 of its 45 years (along with his brother, Jose, who also was a part of the family for 37 years until his retirement in 2022).

"I'll never forget Mr. Elmer," Calderon once said. "I remember one time Mrs. Whitcomb said, 'Elmer, you can't eat that roast beef.' And Mr. Elmer came over one day and said, 'Renee, don't say anything to Mrs. Whitcomb, but I ate some roast beef.'

"He was such a nice man. He treated everyone with such respect, and you felt like part of the family. When you look back at those times [at the Bon-Bon], it was such hard work. We just relied on each other. And now you come to this big office and say, 'Wow.' The sacrifices of those times have really worked."

Over the years, other team members shared similar stories of how the Whitcomb family treated them unlike any other employer they'd known. There was a time when a team member's lung collapsed, and John and Bob visited her in the hospital. Doug often visited a site during a prospective client walk-through and always acknowledged the team for a job well done.

Family often attended weddings, showers, and other momentous occasions in team members' lives. They also attended funerals of team members or members of their family who had passed away.

"I'll never forget when my grandmother died," shared Jennifer (Watson) Dee, a multi-faceted leader in the sales, marketing, and communications departments since 1998 (and one of this book's authors). "I had a huge proposal due that Monday, so I called Paul to tell him of her passing right away. Instead of worrying about how the proposal would get done, he and Doug decided to pass on the prospect and then arranged for their catering team to send a spread of food to my home for after the funeral. Their kindness and generosity spoke volumes that day."

It wasn't uncommon for the Whitcombs to know the names of their team members' spouses and children. And while knowing details and sending funeral care packages may be challenging today in a company of almost 5,000, they still remain genuinely interested in the family and well-being of any member of their team they meet.

"It's important to me to know who I am talking to," said Paul. "I want to shake their hand, know their name, and learn what matters to them. What are they passionate about, how is their family, are they treated right on the job? Everyone contributes to our success—no matter how big this company grows, every individual will always matter."

The extension of this sense of family extends beyond Whitsons' team members. Amid the challenges of business, the family never lost sight of one principal lesson their father taught them: the importance of being of service to others. This became the cornerstone of their business, and it translated down to their teams.

"I remember a significant turning point in my career when I realized just how important our role is in helping others," John shared. "Our team was catering a black-tie event when tragedy struck—a child fell into the pool. One of the workers, tuxedo and all, immediately jumped in and saved this child's life.

"That, to me, was a galvanizing moment and completely indicative of the kind of people that we work with. No matter where you put us, no matter the marketplace, we're all about people."

Countless moments like these have shaped the course of Whitsons' history. Along the way, the spirit of Whitsons was naturally encapsulated into a single, meaningful expression: Enhancing Life One Meal at a Time™.

Whitsons, while synonymous with quality meals, also believed in adding that extra special something to their service. It was this newly defined mission that inspired a change in the family's vision from surviving to thriving.

It was becoming clear that the future of the company lay in contract management—primarily school districts, although corporate dining, senior living, and residential dining, as well as prepared meals, would always play a part. And so the Whitcombs began to seek out and groom the talent that would support the company best in growing those business lines while representing their mission.

Whitsons had finally shaken off the dust of its past and were no longer content simply taking on the clients other contractors had passed on. The Whitcombs began to draw up a plan to tackle the major management companies head-on. Part of that plan would involve looking outside Whitsons for people who could continue to lead the company forward.

One of those people was John Gersbeck. A graduate of Johnson & Wales University in Providence, RI, Gersbeck began his career with a competitor of Whitsons, Ideal Management Services of Ronkonkoma, NY, about 20 miles east of Whitsons' headquarters in Huntington Station.

Because both companies were focusing their contract efforts on school foodservice, Gersbeck had become acquainted with several of the Whitcombs. But it wasn't until he began planning his own wedding that he seriously considered switching companies.

"Whitsons had a major catering presence on Long Island in the 1990s," Gersbeck related. "I met with Kelly [Friend] to see if they could possibly cater our wedding, and we began to talk about business."

Executives at Ideal were looking to sell the company. In Gersbeck's mind, the company had lost focus, becoming more about the bottom line than about serving people, which didn't please the customer-minded Gersbeck.

Friend offered to have someone from Whitsons call him, and Doug placed that call the next day. He invited Gersbeck to come in for an interview. He met with several of the Whitcombs and liked what he saw and heard.

His final meeting was with Friend, and he made a pledge to her: "If you promise to cater my wedding and do a great job, I'll sign a [employment] contract right now."

Gersbeck had one request, however. He didn't want to work as a manager in a school district. So, Whitsons created a supervisory position for him on Long Island.

From there, Gersbeck took on oversight of Whitsons' school accounts in Westchester County... and brought his wife, Karen, also a foodservice management professional, into the mix. As the company began to expand its business into Connecticut and Massachusetts, Gersbeck became the logical choice to relocate to that area and spearhead the process.

"I knew I wanted to work for Whitsons once I walked into the office and viewed all of the Whitcomb family history, memorabilia, and accomplishments. All of the dreams and aspirations that I wanted in my business life have come to fruition since that day. I have said it before, and I will continue to say that I 'bleed green,' just like a member of the Whitcomb family." (Green, in varying shades, has been Whitsons' signature color since its beginnings).

At about the same time as they hired Gersbeck, the Whitcombs realized that it was time for the company to become more technologically savvy. They also knew that there was no one in the house who was skilled enough to take on the task. So, once more, they looked outward, and they found Michael Marinaro.

Marinaro was a self-described computer geek. A graduate of Hofstra University with a degree in business and computer information systems, he answered an ad from Whitsons and came to Huntington to meet with Bob and tour the facility. What he saw was a cobbled-together array of servers stacked on bakers' racks and equipment "scattered everywhere."

Some of the computer equipment was designed for home computer systems, leaving the company extremely vulnerable to attacks from hackers. He knew immediately what needed to be done, and after a second interview a week later, he was given the opportunity.

Within months, he had upgraded the servers, operating systems, switches, and firewalls and installed a rack mount server system. A man who, like the Whitcombs, believed in a strong work ethic, Marinaro installed all of the equipment himself, wrote all the programming, and created all the necessary IP addresses. He then began creating a database using a program called Crunch Time to give Whitsons a leg up on inventory control.

Although he reported to Beth on an organizational chart, Marinaro worked closely with John, and later with Mike, to log all purchased items into the database to allow the company to analyze each business unit more efficiently and effectively.

"I had no food background," Marinaro said. "I didn't know what stuff like a Normandy blend of vegetables was, but I learned very quickly." That knowledge would prove valuable to the company and to Marinaro himself several years later when Whitsons created its first official purchasing department.

But hiring new people was not the only change the growing

company needed; what they also realized was the power of engaging their team members as an active part of the collaboration and vision for the future. To stay current with the trends and truly give customers what they needed, they were going to have to expand their faith and believe in those outside of their inner circle.

One such leap of faith led to the creation of an innovative program focused on healthier eating in schools. Nutrition Safari®, introduced in 2003, is notable for being the first company program that was not conceived or drafted by a Whitcomb family member.

Nutrition Safari was Gersbeck's brainchild, and he and a team composed of Jennifer Dee, Erin Norton, and Holly Von Seggern worked in secret for several months to design the program. Originally called Nutrition On Safari, Nutrition Safari is an educational program aimed at children in kindergarten through sixth grade.

The stars of Nutrition Safari—and the component used to win over the children—are the "animals" that visit the schools. The original characters each represented a different food group and conveyed a different message, from Jillian the Giraffe's "Reach for Your Greens" to Hardy the Hyena's "Hardy, Har, Har, Don't Forget Your Carbs!" Both the animals and the messages were big hits with the students.

The ingenuity behind the program helped Whitsons to stand out in the industry as a company serving more than just a meal—and the recognition followed. In 2008, Nutrition Safari was recognized by *Food Management* with a Best Concept award for Best Wellness Initiative.

What made this program different was its interactivity with the students. Each school received at least one Nutrition Safari visit per year; often, there were more. The visits were conducted by different spokesanimals—actually a Whitsons team member in costume—accompanied by a Safari Ranger who "interprets" the messages from the animal.

"I remember being the original ranger alongside [team member] Melissa Barzcak, who was such a good sport about donning that lion costume in the hot schools," recalled Dee. "We'd literally travel around all of the schools in those early days to spread our message, and to this day, we both recall how special it felt to see those children light up and listen, knowing that we were part of making an impact on their future."

In addition to character visits and messages, Whitsons developed a curriculum that could be used as part of a health class, and monthly nutrition themes and lunch-tasting labs provide hands-on opportunities for students to experience nutrition.

The program has since evolved to phase out old characters and messages and introduce modern spokesanimals that appeal to the newer generation—but the heart of its nutritional awareness foundation still holds true.

"This was an exciting time for the company because the concept came from the team as opposed to ownership," said Paul. "The other cool part is that, all these years later, it still does very well for us because the messages are timeless. They provide the basics of nutritional awareness, and they work in elementary schools because they are fun to learn."

Dee understood the impact this original creation also had on shifting the culture of Whitsons. Beginning as a proposal writing assistant in sales before her leadership in launching and growing Whitsons' official branded marketing and communications departments, she witnessed the company's internal growth from purely family-run to its hybrid of executive-led talent.

"This was the moment when we [team members] knew our commitment to Whitsons was more than loyalty, and we were more than just employees doing some job. Our voices and ideas mattered; we became honorary family members invited to help shape the future of the company. It was really exciting to see and be a part of this change in company dynamics."

The concept of family as a culture began to expand; it was no longer just the Whitcombs and a few long-standing team members who had a part in making the company great. What started out as a simple desire to educate children in health and nutrition led to something even greater: an entrepreneurial spirit.

From here, the Advisory Council Team (ACT) was formed, bringing managers from all walks of the company, from both operations and corporate, together to share ideas, create programs, and birth the innovation that led to Whitsons' continuous, cutting-edge expansion.

"It was something different we were experimenting with," John recollected. "We wanted to open up the opportunity to think outside of our own box. We were hiring people with impressive backgrounds and ideas, and we needed to give them a forum for voicing their creativity."

"I remember asking John and Bob if they were going to be part of the Council," said Friend, who spearheaded the effort. "They were both very clear: they did not want to be there. They wanted to see what could happen when the team felt free to express themselves without 'censorship' or the intimidation that can occur when a company owner was listening."

The result of the team involvement concept was rewarding, leading to ingenious ideas such as peer mentoring and training, team member rewards programs, and trendy menus and promotions.

Since then, the company has opened up to numerous committees and sub-committees to generate creative ideas, from technology advancements and menu concepts to team member wellness events and community outreach initiatives. It seemed like nothing could get in the way of Whitsons' fledgling success.

But as with all progress and anticipation of growth, the Whitcombs realized quickly that success would not come without a cost or without challenges. In fact, the more the company grew, the more complicated the business became. While they had mastered diverse state regulations, they learned that the integrity of their clients was of paramount importance.

There came a point in the summer of 2001 when the company was in serious financial trouble. One client owed them in excess of $1 million—an amount that, at the time, threatened the viability of the business if not recuperated. After multiple attempts to collect, Whitsons found itself resorting to filing a lawsuit, further taxing the already financially distressed business.

The Whitcombs were forced to consider labor cutbacks. They morally struggled with who to furlough and how to deliver this humbling blow in a way that did not alarm its remaining workforce.

"We personally took pay cuts—we weren't being paid," Bob explained. "We were also looking at unprecedented layoffs. Good people, too. Ones we had grown to love like family and who made their individual mark on the company. People who had families of their own would be impacted by this. We knew this was not what our father would have wanted, but what else could we do?"

Taking this drastic measure was something they never wanted, but they had exhausted all other possibilities and financial resources. It was either impact the livelihood of some or the livelihood of all, and the family was not about to let the latter happen.

"It was a very dark time for us," confessed John. "The writing was on the wall. We prayed for a miracle to spare us from what seemed to be an inevitable failure. We just didn't know how we were going to come back from this."

But they didn't have time to worry about that; there were bigger concerns about to plague the nation. Their heavy hearts turned from their financial struggles to a call to service when the terrorist attack, forever after known as 9/11, occurred. New York City needed Whitsons—and their response to the call ultimately spared them and several team members from an untimely downfall.

7.
9/11: A Defining Moment

If there is a focal point for Whitsons, a moment that ultimately defined its business and moral compass, it would have to be September 11, 2001, the day terrorists succeeded in bringing down Manhattan's "Twin Towers" at the World Trade Center. The event both demonstrated the effect of the company's commitment to its clients and proved the contractor's capacity as much as its humanity. It would thrust Whitsons into the role for which it is now most famous.

On that Tuesday morning, Friend, who was then Whitsons' director of operations, and Erin Norton, who had only recently joined the company in the marketing department, were on their way to a meeting off Long Island when the attack on the World Trade Center occurred. They immediately turned around and headed back to the office on Oakwood Road where, Norton recalled, "We all kind of huddled together, ingesting the enormity of it."

There was no television in the office, so employees listened to radio reports from WCBS and WINS. Meanwhile, Doug and Bob were on the phones, calling whoever they could get in touch with, asking what Whitsons could do to help.

They didn't have to wait long. About an hour after the towers fell, Alfred Peck, Director of Homeless Services for the Salvation Army, a Whitsons client since 1987, called Bob and asked if Whitsons could loan the Army two refrigerated trucks "to handle all of the donations we're going to receive."

Bob told Peck they would get right back to him, and Doug did within ten minutes. He agreed to loan the trucks, adding that

Whitsons would do whatever else it could to help in the rescue and relief efforts. Peck promised to arrange a police escort; by this time, all tunnels and bridges leading into Manhattan had been closed. About 15 minutes later, Peck called Doug back, and this time, he asked for 5,000 sandwiches in addition to the trucks.

And the Salvation Army executive wasn't finished; twice more over the next several minutes, he was back on the phone, each time increasing the request: first to 10,000 sandwiches, and then to 25,000.

At that last number, Doug balked. He explained that Whitsons had neither the manpower nor the food to prepare that many sandwiches that quickly. However, for every problem Whitsons—and the Whitcombs—encountered, a solution always seemed to present itself.

In this case, Doug suggested that, instead of more sandwiches, the company would provide 50,000 prepared meals from its culinary centers, which the Army would only have to reheat and serve. Peck jumped at the offer.

After he hung up the phone, Doug called everyone into the board room and explained the situation. Then he asked for volunteers because, in addition to sending prepared meals, Whitsons would be including its Silver Bullet, a large mobile kitchen that is reserved for situations where a temporary production setup is needed.

Every hand in the room rose, so Doug and Bob gave tasks to everyone, assigning them where the brothers thought they would do the most good.

This was not the first disaster Whitsons had been involved with. In September 1985, the company provided relief efforts in the aftermath of Hurricane Gloria, the strongest hurricane to hit Long Island since Hurricane Donna in 1960. Because Long Island Lighting Co. was a Whitsons client, the company provided meals for all LILCO emergency crews, helping to restore power to sections of the island.

The company also assisted the Salvation Army with meals in 1993 when terrorists first tried to blow up the World Trade Center. As Doug was assigning tasks, he believed that Whitsons would once again have a short-term role. He couldn't have been more wrong; 9/11 would prove to be an almost otherworldly experience.

Friend, Brenna Schettino, Robert Papik, and Roger Echauri were in the first group of people selected to go to the disaster site, followed by many other team members who quickly raised their hands to help.

Led by police, the Whitsons team and the Silver Bullet left Oakwood Road early Tuesday evening. There were no cars or trucks on the Long Island Expressway—a surreal event in itself. The same would be true in lower Manhattan, where streets were devoid of moving traffic.

But when the team approached the barricade blocking off Ground Zero, there were thousands of people lined up along the roped-off area, shouting and waving.

"At first, we thought these were the people who needed our help," Friend recalled. "Then we realized that they were all waving photographs. They wanted us to find their loved ones. That was my first 'wow' moment—when the reality of this tragic situation started to sink in."

Indeed, people with relatives or friends who worked in the WTC had printed copies of photos and were handing them out to anyone who would take them. Friend added that when she first began walking around the area, she found herself looking around, half-expecting people to crawl out of the rubble to safety. That was not to be the case, as very few people survived the catastrophe.

"I remember the heat," said Schettino when asked about her initial impressions. "It was warm out that day"—the temperature that day had reached the low 80s—"but this wasn't from the weather. My expectation was that there would be people everywhere, and that wasn't the case.

"There was no line of people waiting to be fed. It was almost quiet, calm, people in fire gear doing what they needed to do. The magnitude of it all was astounding. We were in buildings we probably shouldn't have been in, wading in water up to our knees."

Whitsons set up the Silver Bullet at Chambers Street and the West Side Highway, near Stuyvesant High School and about three blocks from the enormous pile of rubble that was once the Twin Towers. The Salvation Army had stored supplies at the high school, and the Whitsons crew became part of the volunteer team, getting rescue and recovery workers whatever they needed, from a hot meal and bottle of water to clean shirts and socks.

Pallets of food and supplies donated by companies from around the country lined both sides of the West Side Highway. There were clothes, boots, toys, medical supplies—if you could imagine it, someone probably donated it.

Every so often, all work would stop, and there would be silence as another body was pulled from the rubble and transported to one of the makeshift morgues on-site. Schettino said she remembers one particularly poignant moment when a service dog, sent in to search for survivors and bodies, was carried lifeless from the site, another victim of the rescue effort.

Bill and his son, Bill Jr., came into Manhattan by car sometime overnight—time seemed to have little meaning in the initial days after the tragedy—along with brother Andy and then culinary director Robert Jahn, to relieve the first wave of Whitsons team members.

Bill remembers the "heavy snowfall of thick ash, and cars piled five high by heavy equipment" pushed up against buildings on nearly every street. The four men took their places in the Silver Bullet while the others made their way to Bill's car to return to Long Island.

When Schettino returned to Oakwood Road, she became the point person for Whitsons, coordinating the volunteers who were going in to help support the rescue and recovery workers. At the height of the effort, which would continue until the following June, Whitsons would also have serving stations set up at the Medical Examiner's office on First Avenue near NYU Medical Center, at the Fresh Kills Landfill on Staten Island, and at Shea Stadium in Queens.

Whitsons team members behind the scenes at the corporate office and from surrounding accounts continued to aid the mission by packing fresh and frozen meals for the Ground Zero teams to usher in for service. It was an around-the-clock effort with key vendors and partners to keep up with the volume of purchasing, production, and distribution of meals and supplies required to sustain the operation.

Norton took Schettino's place at Ground Zero, and she and Friend managed Whitsons' foodservice efforts in the months to come. It was an emotional time for everyone involved, painful to witness, and yet the Whitsons crew had to hold their emotions in check while on the job.

"We were out on the street with no facilities, no running water, no electricity to speak of, with a big smoldering hole 20 yards away from us," said Friend. "But we couldn't come in and be emotional. We couldn't look these rescue and recovery workers in the face, coming over all filthy, dirty, and exhausted as they were, with anything but a smile. We had to remain professional, smile, and keep making sure everyone was fed safely with the compassion they needed to go back and continue their work."

Bob and MaryLou were among the volunteers working in the Silver Bullet the first few nights. On the day after the attack, Bob noticed that the mobile kitchen's location was allowing it to serve only a small number of the rescue and recovery workers at the site. He decided to head inside the perimeter to see what more could be done.

A US Army MP with an M-16 rifle stopped him at the entrance and directed him to a building along the border where he could apply for a pass. It was late in the evening by the time the Army verified that Bob was working with the Salvation Army, and he was equipped with a pass and a gas mask and allowed to enter Ground Zero.

"It was murky," Bob recalled. "As I entered this space, I experienced a deep emotion of fear and dread because I didn't know what to expect or what I might see. My mind was racing as I made my way through what appeared to me as a dark wasteland with bright lights in the distance."

As he inched closer to the work area, he began to make out the huge cranes and payloaders being used to move massive steel girders into piles. All around were the shattered remains of the buildings that had not collapsed. Inside the lobby of one of these buildings, Bob saw where another caterer had set up a makeshift serving line to feed workers.

"I realized then that we had to relocate inside Ground Zero to really help these guys," Bob said. "That decision transformed how our service would be provided and viewed."

A few days later, Bob and Doug spent the day with a Salvation Army colonel touring Ground Zero. Dressed in full-length coveralls, boots, and face masks, the trio visited all of the service sites that the Army had set up to provide food and clothing for the many rescue workers working the debris pile.

The Army was now coming to grips with the fact that this emergency was far beyond the scope of any previous disaster with which it had been involved. It couldn't handle the task alone, and so the Army turned to Whitsons to transition its temporary setup to an ongoing semi-permanent service.

Over twenty years later, Bob said he could still see in his mind the damage: piles of concrete, crushed cars, and twisted fire trucks, covering everything and hanging in the air a thick powder loaded with asbestos. (In 2018, Bob would be diagnosed with Non-Hodgkin's Follicular Lymphoma; he learned that it could be a result of the time he spent at Ground Zero.)

The scene was unearthly, the destruction hard to comprehend even when seeing it up close. But there was little time to reflect because the goal was to come up with viable foodservice solutions to deal with the complex logistics of Ground Zero.

After the tour was complete, Bob and Doug were taken to the Salvation Army's New York headquarters at 120 West 14th Street in the West Village. They were tired and covered in a mixture of mud and the fine gray powder "that seemed to be everywhere: our eyes, nose, and hair."

They would have liked nothing better than to head home for a hot shower, but they needed to present a plan for managing foodservice over what everyone now realized was going to be at least several months.

Digging into the business side of his brain, Bob had what he considered to be an excellent idea to solve the inefficient service patterns at the various canteens that had been set up. He suggested taking a self-service approach. The colonel's response not only put the entire operation into perspective but also gave

Bob a whole new outlook on customer service, one that he would use to help drive Whitsons forward in the years to come.

"The colonel patiently explained that this was not at all about the food, but about the spiritual care for those being served, the personal touch of one person helping another, in the process reflecting God's love and kindness to the individual," Bob recalled.

"He explained that our food was simply the medium of this important healing process. I was both moved by this matter-of-fact expression and embarrassed for not grasping the obvious spiritual dimensions of this undertaking."

Aside from the enormity—and the gruesomeness—of the task, two challenges faced Whitsons. The more immediate one was the need to meet Department of Health regulations. Despite this being an emergency operation and one cobbled together from many moving parts, food safety standards had to be followed.

Neither Whitsons nor the Salvation Army could afford a food poisoning disaster on top of what had already happened in lower Manhattan. So, portable hand-washing stations were set up for all foodservice workers. Everyone had thermometers to continually check to make sure the hot food and cold food were being held at proper temperatures. Food held for too long outside of accepted temperature zones was disposed of promptly.

Most painfully, the homemade pies, bags of sandwiches, pans of lasagna and baked ziti, and other foodstuffs that hundreds of people brought to the site had to be turned away. Whitsons' staff explained the reasons for their refusal and gave these good Samaritans the names of places where they could take their gifts, information that eased people's disappointment.

There were plenty of opportunities for Whitsons and the Salvation Army to show concern and solidarity and to demonstrate those same traits. One example that Bob related had to do with Whitsons' own mobile kitchen, which was set up the night after the attack.

The kitchen itself was protected by being inside the Silver Bullet's shell. But the other aspects of the serving area were exposed to the elements—including six double-stack convection ovens, modified to use propane, that Whitsons had ordered to meet the increased demand for food.

"There were teams organized by trade: plumbers, electricians, and carpenters, for instance. Their job was to support the people working on the pile," Bob explained. "When one of the carpenters saw what we were doing, he came over and offered to build a lean-to that would shield the ovens and the work area directly surrounding it."

As if that weren't enough, as word spread of what the carpenter was doing, more tradesmen showed up to help. Electricians wired the lean-to so that lights could be installed, and plumbers assisted with the propane hook-ups. The entire structure was fully functional by the end of the day. Over the next few days, Bob heard stories from several other managers about the support they received from these groups.

About two weeks into the recovery operation, Major George Polarek became the director of the Salvation Army's effort in New York City. He and Doug met frequently in the days and weeks that followed. There was a level of trust between the two organizations that went beyond the bounds of contracts, provisos, and indemnifications.

In fact, it created a confidence that transcended the typical red tape that might slow things down. The City would ask the Army for something, and Polarek would say yes. Then he would go to the Whitcombs and relay the request, and they would say yes.

"There wasn't anything that we all wouldn't support if it meant helping the people at Ground Zero," said Doug.

Polarek and Doug discussed the need for a more permanent foodservice site for Ground Zero. A tractor-trailer, delivered from the Salvation Army's operations in Florida, was converted to a full working kitchen, from which thousands of meals per day could be prepared. The trailer and attached serving tent were known as Café Florida. An even better operation would be provided in early December when the Environmental Protection Agency completed the "Taj Mahal," a huge tent that ended up serving as both a changing and decontamination station and a dining hall.

At 35,000 square feet, it had an entranceway large enough to drive an 18-wheeler through. Polarek recalled that when the operations chief for the New York Fire Department walked in the day the tent was opened, he put his hands on his white helmet in amazement. "My God, they'll never want to leave," he said.

Whitsons was able to move into the Taj Mahal because the company was bold enough to stake a claim even before the structure was completed. Team members did a recon of the site and realized that although half the space had been designated for the decontamination area, the other half had yet to be spoken for. So Whitsons had a sign made up and placed it in the center of the space, stating that the area would be taken over by the Salvation Army for "a hospitality environment."

Perception became a reality, and the Army gave Whitsons the task of outfitting the space. Working closely with their suppliers to expedite the delivery of equipment, team members designed that area to accommodate a full kitchen complete with ventilation and fire suppression systems, walk-in refrigerators, serving stations, and a three-basin sink. Outside the kitchen area was a fully carpeted dining hall with seating for 400.

Despite the tremendous work being done by Whitsons and the Salvation Army, not everyone was happy with the arrangement, which created the team's second challenge. Among those complaining were local restaurateurs, whose businesses were suffering, either because their buildings had been damaged or because customers either couldn't or wouldn't come down to lower Manhattan.

From news reports he had seen, Polarek learned that some local businesses were angry that Whitsons, a Long Island company, was the sole provider of food for the rescue and recovery effort. They believed that lower Manhattan restaurants should have been used instead. This resentment was reinforced every time the Health Department shut down a food vendor working outside the perimeter of Ground Zero for food safety violations.

Polarek realized that a plan had to be devised to change this perception. So he and his team sat down with Doug and his team and came up with the Restaurant Revitalization Program (RRP), which kicked off just after Christmas in 2001.

The program operated in two phases. In the initial stage, chefs at affected restaurants would prepare food that would be served in the Taj Mahal. Not only that but each item would be identified on the serving line as having come from a particular restaurant.

Doug would make the overtures to the restaurateurs, Polarek decided; a foodservice operator negotiating with other foodservice operators simply made sense. Whitsons inspected the restaurants to make sure they were able to prepare the meals and that they had certificates of insurance. Whitsons wrote the menus, negotiated a purchase price, picked up the foodstuffs, and stored them until they were needed.

Friend said this gesture was one of her most vivid memories of the time she spent at Ground Zero. "Seeing these grown men, with established restaurants, crying because of this effort was amazing. And then to see them all working together, sharing products and resources, it was like McDonald's shaking hands with Burger King."

During the initial phase of the RRP, Whitsons was not only able to help eateries get back on their feet but also rescue one business' family from squalor. As Friend remembered it, the company learned that the owners of a small Asian restaurant in the zone wanted to be a part of the RRP.

So, Friend led a team to the restaurant, but as soon as they saw the storefront, they knew that the building would need major construction if it were going to be reopened. However, the kitchen, although filled with ash and paper debris, was still intact. But what she also discovered was heart-wrenching. Because their apartment next door had been made unlivable by ash, smoke, and water damage, the owners—father, mother, and five children—had been living in a small section of the kitchen that they had managed to clean up.

Friend connected the family with the Salvation Army for temporary housing. Then, a cleaning crew went in and got the kitchen up and running. Within two days, the family was once again preparing food and, this time, selling it to Whitsons to serve at Ground Zero.

The second phase of the RRP came as a suggestion from New York City Mayor Rudy Giuliani, who asked Polarek to try to come up with a way to encourage people to shop downtown. The Salvation

Army created a system by which volunteers were given vouchers that they could redeem for food at restaurants around Ground Zero. More than 100 restaurants were involved with the program, and between the food they sold to the Army and the vouchers they cashed in from customers, they received nearly $4 million in aid.

Whitsons served its last meal at Ground Zero on May 30, and other sites around the city were also closed over the next several days. The Salvation Army got most of the public credit for the foodservice effort, but Polarek acknowledged that "Whitsons made us look good. Nationally, Whitsons now had a reputation for accomplishing these kinds of things in disaster relief."

For the young foodservice company, it was perhaps the best example of how taking on a client that other contract management firms weren't interested in had paid off in a way no one could have predicted. And virtually all of Whitsons' team members threw themselves into the effort—so much so that after the first week, Bob and Doug had to ration volunteers so that the company itself wouldn't suffer.

Doug remembers one team member who managed to hide from site managers for more than a week because he wanted to continue helping and knew that if he were discovered, his bosses would have made him go home. More than that, the entire time he was volunteering, he had been living out of his truck rather than spending any of the company's money on a hotel room.

That reputation and spirit of service would continue to repeat itself as Whitsons stepped up to help with many more emergency feeding situations in the years to come, such as the devastation left behind by Hurricanes Sandy, Irene, and Katrina, as well as the unprecedented COVID-19 pandemic. Team members would sleep on location during super snowstorms to ensure residents received their daily meals, and drivers creatively found alternate routes to keep on delivering meals to affected communities.

But as much as Whitsons' team may have gotten out of their humanitarian gestures in emergency service, the post-9/11 work, in particular, still deeply affected many of them in ways they weren't even aware of. That became evident several months after the fact when a representative from Project Liberty called Schettino.

Project Liberty, a joint effort between the Federal Emergency Management Agency and the Center for Mental Health, wanted to counsel Whitsons team members who might be suffering from Post-Traumatic Stress Disorder. Schettino's first response was no; how could anyone at Whitsons have PTSD? But the representative was insistent that PTSD can manifest itself in many ways.

So Schettino relented and agreed to have someone from Project Liberty visit the office. However, she would have to beg and cajole people to "just show up" because, like herself, no one at Whitsons thought they needed counseling. Many reluctantly agreed to sit in a conference room "for ten minutes" to hear what the counselor had to say. Two hours later, not a soul had left that room. The stories and the tears poured forth, and team members began to heal from the trauma, the feelings, and the nightmares they didn't know they had kept bottled up.

Like so many others, the tragedy of 9/11 that tore so many lives apart also brought so many others together in unity. For the team at Whitsons, they would forever be changed by the events they witnessed. As a company, it would teach them who they were as people, as a family, and as a community, and it restored hope for a new kind of future, one that they'd never take for granted again.

Photos in Time

Where it All Began: Elmer & Gina

The Whitcomb Family Through the Years

Top Row: Doug, Diane, Mike, Andy, Kevin Smith, Laurie, MaryLou, Bob, Bill, John
Bottom Row: Beth, Elmer, Gina, Paul

Top Row: Doug, Diane, John, Danny, Paul, Laurie, MaryLou, Bob
Bottom Row: Bill, Carolyn, Beth, Jean, Mike

**All photos from family and company archives

A Family Grows

Top Row: Bob, John, Paul, Bill, Mike, Andy, Doug
Bottom Row: Joe Daly, Gina, Beth, Laurie

Top Row: Mary, Mike, Jean, Andy, Danny, Joanna, Paul, Carolyn, John, Diane, Doug, Bob
Bottom Row: Tony, Amanda, Susan, Beth, Gina, Joe, Michell, Bill

2023: Celebrating Gina's 96th birthday with 4 generations of Whitcombs

**All photos from family and company archives

The Evolution of a Business

Original Bon-Bon sign and menu in 1979

The Silver Bullet days at Kaufman Astoria Studios' Commissary (team pictured with Harrison Ford while filming "Sabrina")

Huntington Commissary production line (right)

The first official office at Oakwood Road in Huntington in 1996 (below)

Whitsons' first fleet (bottom)

**All photos from family and company archives

Building Upon a Dream

Paul and Doug reviewed plans for the renovation of the new office and culinary center in Islandia

Islandia Headquarters ready for occupancy in 2006

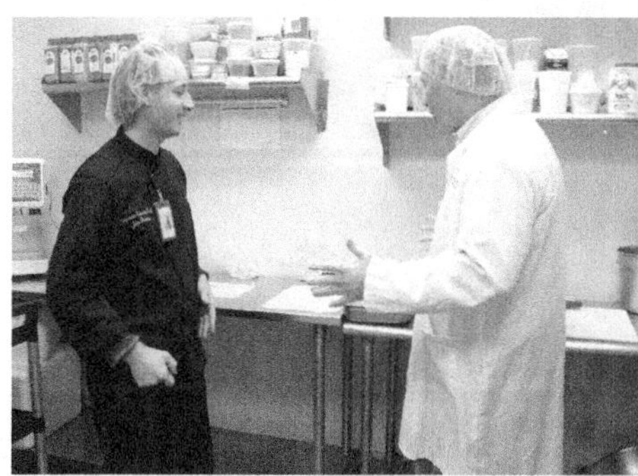

John Koutras and Bob Whitcomb make plans for the USDA Culinary Center

Bob, Bill, John, and Mike proudly reveal fleet upgrade

**All photos from family and company archives

The Tragedy of 9-11

Whitsons team Kelly Friend, Erin Norton, and Dan Cramer posing with rescue workers (above)

Jumping into service on West Street on 9/12 (left)

The many faces of those we served (below)

Food operations in the EPA tent, affectionately called "The Taj"

**All photos from family and company archives

The Tragedy of 9-11

Erin Norton presenting then Mayor Rudy Giuliani with a Whitsons jacket

Doug Whitcomb with Major George Polarek and members of the Salvation Army

The Silver Bullet in action (above)

One of many heartfelt letters that came from schools across the country (right)

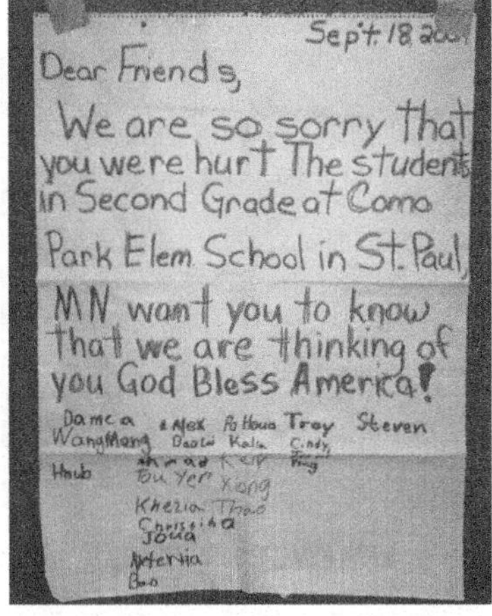

Sept. 18 2001

Dear Friends,

We are so sorry that you were hurt The students in Second Grade at Como Park Elem. School in St. Paul, MN want you to know that we are thinking of you God Bless America!

Troy Steven

Whitsons and the Salvation Army partnered with local businesses as part of its Restaurant Revitalization Program

Catering Highlights

Kelly Friend with Frank Purdue in 1993

Setting up for a beautiful wedding at Coindre Hall in 2002

Andy's famous clambake

Andrews' mobile kitchen setup at Jets Training Center

Kelly and Andy with Fabulous Foods' chefs in early 1990s

Joseph Daly, Eric Redlich, and Craig Whitcomb at the grill

**All photos from family and company archives

The Many Looks of On-Site Service

School contract management all began here: Hicksville High School in 1992

The Cafe at Kaufman Astoria Studios

The evolution of our Signature Series branded stations

Today's Real Meals' look in elementary schools (left); Pop-Up Shop promo (bottom)

**All photos from family and company archives

Through the Years: Contract Management

The "Whitsons Cares" team building an obstacle course at Madonna Heights in 2001 (l-r): Mike Whitcomb, Mark Tammone, Chris Fautas, Bob Whitcomb, John Gersbeck, Paul Whitcomb, John Whitcomb

John and Chef Andy at an early '00s Culinary Expo

Bill represents for the roll-out of "Wild Bill's Burger Canyon"

On the Huntington School lunch line with Kelly Friend, Andy Whitcomb, and Christine "CKW" Kunnmann

John Whitcomb, John Gersbeck, Jeffrey Taddeo, Rich Sandmann, and Jennifer Syrowsky at an MA Expo

Fred Hakimi, Kelly Friend, Mark Kirn, and Peter Bellisario with his team at St. Christopher Ottilie residence

**All photos from family and company archives

Nutrition Safari launches at New Britain with original Ranger Jennifer "Dr. Watson" Dee and Luke the Lion

Meet the Characters: Heidi the Hippo, Jillian the Giraffe, Luke the Lion, Hardy the Hyena, Murray the Monkey, and Grant the Gazelle

The 2003 Culinary Expo launch of the award-winning nutrition program

The CM Real Meals launch team: (l-r) Shannon Nemethy, Melissa Hepple, Jeffrey Taddeo, Elizabeth Sunbury, and Chef Tyrell Jones

The original guest chef Rich Sandmann and his famous Sushi Flats

**All photos from family and company archives

Through the Years: Prepared Meals

Veteran team members Emmitt Smith (top left) and Lisa Torrez (bottom left)

The Huntington prepared meals teams in 1997 (above left) and 2002 (below)

The Islandia team in 2008

Laurie loved to spread joy

Chef Bobby Jahn

Ribbon cutting ceremony for Elizabeth, NJ center in 2007

A hard working team celebrates a Boston win

**All photos from family and company archives

The Islandia team achieves SQF certification in 2015

David Smith leads the team in a management meeting

Chef Peter Johnson deep in his Real Meals R&D

Holiday Party 2022

Krisztina Subic with Paul Whitcomb

**All photos from family and company archives

Memories and Moments

Bill Whitcomb and crew at a team member picnic

District Managers in the early school years: Christopher Gagnon, Renee Lotvin, and Chris Fautas

Team building fun in 2002 (above)

The Huntington corporate crew in 1998 (left)

Brenna Schettino, Doug Whitcomb, and Nancy Yates at a team member picnic

John Gersbeck and Mike Whitcomb at the Huntington office

Doug Whitcomb with Michael Marinaro at a team event

**All photos from family and company archives

The whole management team at Whitsons' 2004 Night of the Stars

Party-goers Christine Kunnmann, Chris Gagnon, Renee Lotvin, Steve Schleifer, Chris Fautas, John Gersbeck, Mark Tammone, and Tony Aguanno

Beth presents Laura Gaglione with an award

Bob is honored with the IFMA 2009 Silver Plate Award

Beth is recognized by the American Heart Association

Chris Neary presents Andy with the 2008 ACF Chef of the Year

Team members from all areas of service join together to take a photo in honor of Whitsons' 35th anniversary in 2014

Craig Whitcomb, Karen Scott, and Gina Lombardi

**All photos from family and company archives

The sales and operations teams at a client dinner in New Jersey

Patricia Spence-Kotch, Mary DiStefano, Karen Dittrich, and Katherine Frielingsdorf collect gifts for SCO

Service during the time of COVID-19

Ready for an emergency (l-r): Tony DiStefano, Paul Burnup, Beth Bunster, Paul Whitcomb, Paul's son Niko, Mike Whitcomb, and David Smith

At the Baylor Collaborative Hunger Summit (l-r): Paul Whitcomb, David DeScenza, Paula Presley, Jennifer Dee, Kelly Friend, and Ozzie Orsillo

Bill Whitcomb, Jr. and John Gersbeck usher in a new wave of leadership (above)

The end of an era: brothers Jose and Renee Calderon retire with Gina Whitcomb-Daly (left)

**All photos from family and company archives

8.
The New Millennium: Schools

Although the months following the World Trade Center attack seemed to consume Whitsons, company business did continue as usual—and in the meantime, they successfully won their lawsuit and reclaimed their million-dollar-plus income as contracted. They were finally able to put that battle behind them and focus on their renewed future as true service providers.

By 2002, Whitsons was a $60-million company and school accounts were responsible for the bulk of that revenue. So, in the summer of 2002, with the work of Ground Zero finally behind them, the Whitcombs turned almost all of their attention to expanding the business outside of New York and New Jersey.

They set their sights on New England.

Gersbeck, who had relocated from Long Island, was now spending virtually all of his time in Connecticut, trying to entice school clients to buy into Whitsons' game plan. Gersbeck found it to be a tough sell; the incumbent contractors, Aramark and Sodexo, were two of the three largest contract companies in the world, and they had resources to burn.

So, as the company had done for all of its life, Whitsons aimed for smaller districts, ones that most other companies wouldn't give a second glance. Marketing itself as the company that could offer hands-on treatment of its clients from top executives, Whitsons began to catch the ear of a few districts.

Because of its past experience with its B&I accounts, Whitsons developed a business model that was different from the way most large, global companies went to market. Whitsons brought a retail focus to the business and found a way to pitch that focus even in the face of bids that had to be calculated down to the penny.

"We're closer to the ground," Gersbeck said. "We look through a different lens and see revenue opportunities that other people can't see."

The non-institutional approach had been embraced by other regional contractors, but no one in the New York/New Jersey/Connecticut market was doing it except Chartwells, the education services arm of Compass Group North America. "We bashed heads a lot because we have similar programs," he admitted.

In 2002, when the company won the bid over Sodexo for Brookfield Public Schools in Connecticut, one could have understood if Sodexo executives shrugged their shoulders. After all, with only two elementary schools, a middle school, and a high school, Brookfield wasn't exactly a huge money-maker for the Gaithersburg, MD-based contractor.

But in 2003, when Whitsons won several additional school accounts—also from Sodexo—people took notice. This was the largest growth spurt in the state. As such, it was a big deal; on opening day, Bob, then CEO, was there in his short sleeves, spreading the dough to make pizzas.

Although this was an exciting time for the Whitcombs, there was still another lesson waiting to be learned. They underestimated the challenges associated with introducing their new, innovative ideas and processes to an existing, close-knit community comfortable with their own tried-and-true methods of practice.

It became clear for one account in particular that their goals were no longer aligned, and the district was not receptive to the improvements the company wanted to make. Unfortunately, even after trying to find mutual ground, Whitsons made the difficult decision to end the partnership.

Gersbeck would later consider this a turning point for the company. "At first, I took it as a failure," he said. "But then I realized that the company was now strong enough to be willing to end relationships with accounts that were not a good fit. We want great partnerships. If it's one-sided, it doesn't work."

Whitsons' unorthodox approach to schools helped it win another large Connecticut district, New Britain, in 2004. Administrators there didn't know exactly what to make of Whitsons' proposal, so they arranged a surprise visit to another of Whitsons' accounts, the Mount Vernon School District in Westchester County, NY.

"As it so happened, I was at the district the day they visited," said Gersbeck. "I walked out of the high school, and there was a coach bus outside with about 15 people from New Britain getting off. I took them to visit a couple of schools. They liked what they saw, and we won the bid."

New Britain, with over 10,000 students, is one of Whitsons' biggest success stories. Jeffrey Taddeo, another team member who came from a competitor, was the resident district manager at New Britain since the day Whitsons took over the account up until his promotion as a district manager for the Connecticut region. Under his guidance, the program became so highly thought of that seven other private schools in the New Britain area became part of the district's foodservice program, giving Whitsons a total of 22 locations in and around the city.

Taddeo became an active member of the community, volunteering his time at the New Britain Boys and Girls Club. It was actually as a result of his involvement with that organization that he came up with the idea for the district's dinner program, which was run out of the Boys and Girls Club and for which Whitsons donated the equipment.

The out-of-the-box thinking by Taddeo and the New Britain team inspired multiple pilot programs for other Whitsons accounts, including highlighting local farm partnerships, staging research and development for new branded menu concepts, and employing individuals from community organizations that help young adults with disabilities seek meaningful careers.

Over the next decade, with Gersbeck in the lead and customer-focused managers such as Taddeo carrying the ball day-to-day, Whitsons would repeat the New Britain story in districts such as Hamden, East Haven, Norwalk, Fairfield, and many more. In East Haven, Gersbeck discovered Rich Sandmann, a foodservice director with a passion for food and the chef skills to match, a happenstance that led to one of Whitsons' most popular programs.

Sandmann was the foodservice manager for Sodexo at East Haven, and he and his district manager did not get along. When Whitsons took over the East Haven account, Sandmann sought out Gersbeck because he felt he had no future at Sodexo. Gersbeck saw that Sandmann could be an asset to the company, and so he recommended that Whitsons hire him. How much of an asset would become more clear over the next few years.

Sandmann's first job with the company was supposed to be as the assistant director in New Britain, but administrators in East Haven valued Sandmann so much that they convinced Gersbeck to let him stay on there. So Sandmann worked at East Haven for another three years until Gersbeck had a brainstorm.

Until around 2010 or so, chefs were a rarity in school foodservice, a fact that did not escape Gersbeck's notice. The challenge was how to make the best use of Sandmann's ability. In 2005, Gersbeck went to John Whitcomb and proposed the creation of a visiting chef program for schools, with Sandmann as the man to display his culinary skills in front of students at lunchtime. Gersbeck had already floated the idea past Sandmann, who was thrilled.

"I thought it was an awesome idea, absolutely incredible," Sandmann recalled. "I saw what was happening with Whitsons and their vision of what school foodservice could be, and it was totally different from my old company. I would have the chance to show people that school food didn't have to be chicken nuggets and tater tots, that we had a lot more to offer."

John gave the concept his blessing, and soon Sandmann was traveling throughout the state, presenting to students upscale versions of Whitsons' concepts, such as La Cucina and Coyote Grill. The goal was two-fold: to get students to try new types of foods and to empower team members to become more creative in serving and engaging with their customers.

After communicating ahead of time with the director at the targeted school district, Sandmann typically would arrive around 6 or 6:30 am on the day of the event. Usually, his ingredients and supplies would be set up already. Sandmann would get to work laying out the appropriate decor and organizing the line for the best presentation to students. When the lunch periods began,

Sandmann would be out there, preparing the day's specialty to order for students.

"Visuals are huge," Sandmann said. "We try to cook on the line as often as we can. When you get those smells in the air, along with the visuals, everything starts working."

Sandmann admitted that the first few months were "quite the challenge." First, in most cases, he had never been to the district, so he was flying blind in terms of the layout of the kitchen and the available equipment. "In the early days, every visit was like an episode of MacGyver," he said, alluding to the television series from the late 1980s in which the hero would create all sorts of homemade gadgets to solve problems and rescue people.

"I would call ahead and speak with the directors, ask them what equipment they had, and then I would get there and find out something wasn't working. So we would have to back up and figure out how to make the event work, like steaming pasta versus boiling it."

In true Whitsons fashion, Sandmann improvised well and learned quickly from his mistakes; for example, after one near-disastrous sushi demonstration—the rice steamer was down, so the sushi rice had to be boiled—he went out and bought two portable rice cookers so he'd not be caught off-guard again. But over time, the kinks were ironed out, and the program is as popular now as it was 20 years earlier—adding more visiting chefs into the mix throughout Whitsons' various regions.

As the first decade of the millennium moved along and Connecticut became more of a Whitsons stronghold for school foodservice, the company looked farther north, into Massachusetts. To help Gersbeck in this effort, Whitsons hired its first team member from Massachusetts, Ozzie Orsillo.

Orsillo, another of those salespeople who had crossed paths with one or more Whitcombs over the years, began his career working for Servomation Corp. Over time, through mergers and acquisitions, he wound up working for Compass Group. His role with Compass was in school foodservice sales, which pitted him against Paul when he was vying for business in Connecticut.

Orsillo, who is now Whitsons' senior vice president of strategy and growth, explained that he came to like Paul as a person and was intrigued with the family aspect of the business, as well as how the company operated.

"I just had an 'a-ha' moment one day when I was in a board room in Miami, Florida, listening to the corporate folks telling us how things needed to be," Orsillo recalled. "I thought to myself that if I was going to do this job for the rest of my life, I didn't want to do it like this."

So he started a conversation with Paul, and Whitsons offered him the chance to switch companies. With Gersbeck and Orsillo working in tandem, business in Massachusetts began to take off. By 2016, Whitsons would have 24 accounts in the Bay State—six of them earned in just one year.

In 2011, in the midst of that eight-year run, Whitsons' position as a leader in the school foodservice world was firmly established when it won the bid to provide prepared meals to 86 schools in the Boston Public School system. (In 2011, Boston had two distinct foodservice programs. At 44 schools that have full-service cafeterias, district foodservice staff prepared and served meals. But for the rest of the district's locations, frozen prepared meals were delivered to the schools and reheated on-site.)

This would be an entirely new experience for the company. Not only would Boston be its largest school account by far, but it would also be the only district where Whitsons would not be preparing any meals from scratch on-site. The contract would also tax the growing prepared meals division.

As Gersbeck explained it, "Although in places like New Britain we satellited meals from one location to other schools, this was going to be 20 times more than that. We were talking about 30,000 meals per day: breakfast, lunch, and snack." Adding to the challenge was the transportation element; with no culinary centers in Massachusetts, Whitsons would have to ship meals to Boston from New York.

Still, Mike believed this opportunity aligned with Whitsons' vision for expanding its presence in the marketplace. "We were already growing our school nutrition business in New England, so introducing prepared meal services was a natural progression—

especially with the success we were simultaneously experiencing in other states. We knew we had the resources and capabilities to support the program. We just needed to find a way to get our foot in the door."

That would be easier said than done. The bid process for the contract was contentious. For the previous six years, the prepared meals contract had been held by Preferred Meal Systems (PMS) of Berkeley, IL. When Boston released its latest request for proposals—contracts are awarded in Massachusetts every three years—the RFP came under fire from other bidders, who felt that the language in the proposal favored PMS. Another competitor even sent a four-page letter to the district detailing the reasons why it was declining the opportunity to submit a bid.

The outcry caused administrators to redraft the contract. Among the additions was a recommendation that bidders pledge to try "increasing fresh fruit and vegetable purchases from local farmers."

The amendment also dovetailed nicely with the sustainability initiatives that were occurring at Whitsons. In 2009, the company implemented the Greenleaf Cuisine local purchasing initiative as part of a comprehensive environmental program that included Taskforce Green, a conservation program, as well as an initiative to begin using vehicles that ran on biodiesel fuel. In its presentation, Whitsons made it known that the company would be willing to install salad bars in schools to complement the pre-packaged meals—a winning move on the company's part.

But that's not all that went into securing the contract. According to Mike, the decision to award the bid to Whitsons came down to multiple factors, including a strong regional team, established partnerships with local growers, and a taste test that all but clinched the deal. "In the end, it is about the food," he explained. "You can't serve food to people that you don't enjoy yourself. They [the Boston evaluation committee] loved the quality and taste of our meals and decided we were the best fit to feed their community."

After Whitsons won the bid, the company secured a warehouse in the city to which it would ship the meals from New York. Drivers would then deliver the meals to individual schools. This presented a new challenge for Gersbeck: how to deal with the drivers who, understandably, were concerned that they might be replaced. Whitsons, however, was not interested in replacing veteran drivers in a city with which it was unfamiliar.

So, Gersbeck involved the drivers in the takeover process. He sat down with every driver individually and asked him or her about their schedules. What time did they normally hit the road? How long did it take to reach their destinations? Then, Gersbeck's team drafted a schedule based on the information they had gathered, and the drivers were satisfied. When the contract went out for bid again in 2014, Whitsons retained the business.

Around the same time, Doug's son Craig was called upon to help expand the business into New Jersey and Pennsylvania—christened quickly into the world of school nutrition with the challenge of opening one of the largest urban school districts in New Jersey with only ten business days' notice.

"I am still not sure how we pulled it off," Craig explained, "but somehow, we managed to acclimate and train 370 new team members, place and receive orders, overcome equipment and service shortages, and communicate with the community—all before the start of the school year."

The feat was accomplished thanks to team members who came together from three different states, proving once again that anything is possible for the Whitsons team. Their efforts led to several years of financial stability for the district and served as a turning point for continuing expansion and making a name for Whitsons in yet another growing region.

Not only was the school nutrition business expanding, but other contract management opportunities were presenting themselves, including healthcare institutions, long-term care facilities, and on-site residential dining programs. Though smaller in scale than school districts, Whitsons found its place in these markets as they specialized in various dietary requirements and patient dining needs—combining all their years of diverse operational knowledge into an ability to adapt to practically any kind of on-site dining environment.

The burgeoning industry leader thus shifted from a trial-

and-error mindset to diligently aligning with the right partners with matching visions. That, combined with having a better understanding of how to blend relationship development with distinct regional bidding strategies, positioned Whitsons to build its reputation for integrity and excellence as it entered its next decades of service—where it now serves educational, residential, and healthcare dining programs in more than 13 states.

9.
The New Millennium: Prepared Meals

If schools were the main segment upon which Whitsons would build its contract management business, prepared meals would become a point of differentiation between Whitsons and other foodservice contractors.

The prepared meals business, which had been incubating since that first near-fateful mayor's luncheon in Astoria in 1987, was ready to advance to the next level. After outgrowing the studio commissary, post office hub, and Queens location, operations and opportunities really solidified when the company opened its own kitchen on Oakwood Road in Huntington Station, NY.

"Before Oakwood, there was no centralized location or system," explained Bob. "What we had was a series of kitchens that cooked and packaged meals on-site, each prepared to be served to the customers closest to them. But we needed something more if we were going to seriously pursue this business and be successful."

Heading into the millennium at the new facility, the prepared meals sector experienced its first wave of true market growth. Whitsons' presence expanded into the Mid-Atlantic and even marked its foray into the world of long-term healthcare, where they learned the unique ins and outs of JCAHO certification, patient dining and nutrition standards, and specialty medical diets. And yet, that was just the beginning.

As this part of the business grew, Whitsons began opening more production facilities, which it referred to as culinary centers. In 2002, the company opened the Bronx Culinary Center. This 8,000-square-foot facility allowed the company to service new accounts in senior nutrition, as well as daycare centers and homeless shelters.

Two years later, Whitsons did the same thing in Queens, opening the Queens Culinary Center. Out of this 5,000-square-foot production area, the company began to provide service for all of its New York City clients while also expanding its services to more senior programs, daycare centers, and homeless shelters in that borough.

"Adding these culinary centers was important for growth," Mike explained. "We knew we had a good product and that customers loved our meals, but what was missing were more local distribution centers that would support expansion into new states. Having a physical presence in these regions opened up more than just convenient delivery; as a company, we experienced better economies of scale, were able to support emergency meal service during disasters to more areas, and they helped us prepare for the next step: new markets and eventually, USDA standards."

During this time of culinary center expansion, Fautas returned to the prepared meals side of the business at the production center on Oakwood Road, helping to diversify its opportunities. This is when thinking outside of the box became more of the norm than the exception for the company, as it continued to try different avenues—some successfully, some not as much.

One of those next levels was preparing meals using what is known as a cook-chill method. The benefit of this method is maintaining the quality, nutrition, and freshness of a scratch-prepared meal while naturally preserving it. This enabled Whitsons to increase its production capabilities while maintaining a high level of quality service.

In its determination to serve a better end product to all customers, Whitsons even began working with Tyson to brand its own "Whitsons chicken," offering pre-packaged, solid white, fully cooked breasts in both grilled and breaded varieties to its contract management accounts.

By 2006, the Oakwood Road office and production center were bursting at the seams, pushing Whitsons to make its most significant move to date. The Whitcombs acquired a 54,000-square-foot warehouse in Islandia, about 20 miles east of Huntington. Here, Fautas was given the job of coordinating the move of the culinary center business "without disrupting customer service," he was told.

According to Fautas, the challenge was: How could they move operations to the new center but still run the business during the one-week transition with the Oakwood location closed? The solution was to use off-site refrigerated trailers on a rented lot nearby. With everything up to code, service went off without a hitch.

"It was unlike anything we ever expected," said Fautas, "but we pulled through, and not a single customer program was disrupted. What we were able to accomplish as a team was pretty impressive."

Moving from Huntington to Islandia was "a major leap" in terms of size, according to Bob. Formerly a McDonald's distribution center, the building already had some refrigeration in place, and the freezer alone was as large as the entire Huntington building had been.

Team member Lisa Torrez, who has been with the company for 24 years, can remember her start in the one-room operation in Huntington Station.

"When I joined the team at Huntington, it was small," said Torrez. "It only had like ten people. Everything was manual. No machines. One computer. We made the meal in one place and then sealed the plate by hand.

"I remember many times when I was working, Mr. Robert and Mrs. Beth would come on the line and ask, 'How do you work so fast like that?' They said they had never seen anyone work like that before. Especially because we had to do it all ourselves with few tools and equipment—but I knew I just had to get it done for our customers. And so whenever we got a new client, everyone was like, 'Give it to Lisa to open.'"

"Lisa is sharp and lightning quick," added Bob. "There wasn't anything we couldn't give her that she couldn't handle. She became the heart of our team, and her commitment continues to lead us to success today."

Torrez was among the team that helped transition the business from Oakwood to Islandia—a space ten times larger than the team was used to working in.

As such, the family faced a tough question: What did they want to do with all that space? The prepared meals business was still small potatoes compared to the contract business. However, this new space could give the company what it needed to move to the next level—if the Whitcombs were willing to commit the money and resources.

"Going from Oakwood Road to Islandia changed everything," said Paul. "We were facing real risks because the move brought with it much higher fixed costs. There was a lot of conversation among our family about whether this was the right move. How much more business would we have to sell? What would happen if we don't sell enough business? It was a daunting decision, to say the least."

But the family ultimately decided that there was enough potential in prepared meals for them to take the chance. And it was a smart move in terms of space. At long last, they reasoned, the prepared meals division would have room to grow.

And so, the company transitioned from Huntington, with basic kettle and tilting skillets, to a proper production facility with blend therms, automated packaging, and overwrap machines to support a more complex production system. Whitsons would be able to go from making only 30- to 40-gallon batches of sauce to preparing 300-gallon or larger quantities of sauce at a time. Packing meals, at the time being done in aluminum trays with paper lids crimped on, could now be accomplished more efficiently and safely in trays with heat-sealed covers.

But this didn't come quite as easily as the Whitcomb family had anticipated. Enter yet another learning curve.

When Whitsons built the Islandia facility, they built it with the knowledge and experience that they had to date, which was not large-scale manufacturing—it was catering. So, it was designed more like an expanded catering facility. What they had yet to understand were the USDA processes and what they really required from a facility. The processes, the equipment, and the sanitation standards—becoming aligned with these new standards became yet another hurdle Whitsons had to overcome.

"We learned something critical about sanitation," Paul revealed. "Sanitation isn't about how you clean, although that's part of it. It's about how the facility and equipment are designed. A facility has to be designed to be sanitary, and then you can clean it accordingly. But if it's not, there is nothing you can do to keep it logistically sanitary. We had to modify the facility to be compliant, efficient, and ready for our intended growth."

Krisztina Subic, vice president of planning and production, has been part of the continuous development of the production and assembly areas of the Islandia Culinary Center for the last 14 years. She has witnessed several iterations of the facility design as the company evolved through client services and markets, learning through a lot of trial and error.

"In the beginning, I remember when the kitchen and production room in Islandia were close together, and we were packing food not far from where we created the labels," Subic shares. "In the Oakwood facility, under local Board of Health conditions, this was a completely acceptable practice. But for the USDA? We had to adjust our layout multiple times until we got it right."

By learning and making important design changes, the company could finally achieve what it desperately needed to grow this division: a USDA-inspected facility, which happened later that first year. Not long after that, Whitsons sought accreditation by two Global Food Safety Initiative-approved (GFSI) standards that outlined safety, quality, and operational criteria for retail food producers and suppliers: the British Retail Consortium (BRC) and Safe Quality Food (SQF).

By the mid-2000s, with a USDA inspector "in the house" and official BRC and SQF certifications—along with a solid team committed to Whitsons' mission and the space and resources to modernize operations—Whitsons was able to sign its first contract to produce meals for a retail brand and take on a new business venture.

At this time, the diet craze had fully engulfed the country. The Zone Diet, South Beach Diet, and others attracted the eyes of entrepreneurs who believed they could marry the desire of

Americans to eat more healthfully with their apparent disdain for cooking at home by creating meal delivery services. While the fledgling division produced meals for several diet program start-ups, none proved to have a sustainable model.

In 2006, Whitsons was approached by one of those dietary start-ups, a Queens company called Nu-Kitchen. The company prepared healthy meals, packaged them, and delivered them fresh every day to about 1,000 customers in the New York metro area.

Nu-Kitchen was, in the Whitcombs' estimation, a grand idea except for the fact that the owners were inexperienced in the food production side of the business. As a result, they weren't making any money. They asked Whitsons to take over the production and fulfillment, using Nu-Kitchen's recipes.

Except, there were no recipes. John Koutras, an innovative culinary research and development specialist and operational leader for Whitsons over the last 18 years—now senior vice president of operations for prepared meals—clearly remembered the complexity of developing this program practically from scratch.

"When we started Nu-Kitchen, I went down to their Long Island City Culinary Center with a tape recorder because we had no recipes yet. And then, before they grabbed the salt, I'd tell them to stop and weigh the salt. I didn't want to stop them just cooking by hand, but I did want to weigh the before and after so we could develop a recipe for every single menu item on-site."

This level of tediousness delayed the project quite a bit. When the program was ready to launch, Marinaro recalled it was an "all hands on deck" effort by the entire Whitcomb family and corporate office team to pack meals throughout the night before the first distribution was scheduled.

"I remember it was on a Sunday night—mainly because Bob and I talked about how we were missing the season finale of *The Sopranos* that night to make it happen," Marinaro joked. "But we were short-staffed. We all came together as a team because it was important; the family's success was our success."

According to Fautas, Bob was running around with candy bars for everyone that evening, to the dismay of the vending team, who were none too happy the next day with the disappearance of their inventory. But it was all in the name of keeping spirits up and getting a tough job done.

Whitsons ran this program for about three years. Every day, there was a different choice of menu items—usually two—packaged in large and small sizes or, as is generally thought of, 'male' and 'female' portions. Whitsons would prepare, package, and label the meals. Then, they would be organized by zip code and delivered to Whitsons' depot in Queens, where drivers contracted by Nu-Kitchen would pick up the packages and deliver them.

What Whitsons prepared was "high-quality, always fresh, never frozen," but the logistics were complicated. Production numbers were staggering: 10,000 pounds of mashed potatoes, 20,000 pieces of grilled chicken, etc. Inevitably, due to the short window between order and delivery, food waste occurred. Whitsons had to forecast orders so it could buy ingredients. When Nu-Kitchen's owners sold the business to Nutrisystem in 2008, Whitsons continued to provide the same service until the Whitcombs realized the service had peaked and was no longer sustainable.

At roughly the same time as its deal with Nu-Kitchen, Whitsons contracted with another start-up, called e-Diets, to run a similar program. This time, however, Whitsons was asked to develop the recipes for the program as well as prepare the meals. e-Diets was different from Nu-Kitchen in that meals were packaged in a modified atmosphere, frozen, and delivered to customers once a week.

Business grew substantially over a four-year period to the point where Whitsons was preparing a week's worth of meals for about 3,000 customers, or about 63,000 meals in total. However successful the service was, the customer acquisition costs were so high that e-Diets still wasn't able to make money. e-Diets eventually went out of business.

In both cases, the start-ups offered Whitsons the opportunity to buy them out, but the Whitcombs were not interested in acquiring those businesses. However, they had gotten a taste of this new market and would eventually set out to develop their own branded products.

Meanwhile, the company had transitioned to a central

production model for some of its prepared meals business. This included some school districts, as well as Meals-on-Wheels programs and daycare centers. Whitsons made IPMs (individually portioned meals) in Islandia and delivered them to its culinary centers in the Bronx, Queens, and, eventually, Elizabeth, NJ, where they were combined with sides (milk, bread, butter, and fruit, for instance) and delivered.

Menu items for congregate sites such as senior centers and homeless shelters were prepared in bulk, also in Islandia, and delivered to local culinary centers to be distributed from there. The company continued to invest in additional, larger equipment, not only to produce more meals but to be able to make different types of meals at the same time. By providing more variety to clients, Whitsons became more flexible while still maintaining an efficient operation.

This consolidation process was very complex and required the implementation of rigorous production techniques and sound sanitation procedures. It also meant a complete devotion to the continuous improvement process in order to be successful.

One significant example of this was the decision to transition from a manual process to a Material Requirements Planning [MRP] system called X3, designed to fully automate end-to-end production and quality control standards with system redundancies.

"We needed better control of what we bought and made," Beth explained about the decision to invest in the new technology. "We were too manual and Excel-based. It worked for a while—until it didn't. We could have kept doing what we were doing if that's all we wanted to do. But to go beyond where we were, we had to take a giant leap.

"Before then, it was a little improvement here, a little improvement there, and so on. And then the business got so big that we couldn't just keep making little improvements. We had to decide to either stay where we are or take that risk for something better."

And that leap is where some businesses fail. A radical system change of this nature is traditionally a huge expense requiring enormous commitment, patience, and the ability to push through complicated challenges while still conducting regular business.

"It was so brutal, we almost quit midway," said Beth. "We didn't know if we could see the end of it. I didn't know if it was worth it anymore. It was like an onion; every time we peeled back a layer, another would appear and complicate matters more."

"Everybody was trying to tell me not to do it for a while. But we had to do it," Bob believed. That's when he knew he had to pull Marinaro into the picture and find out what they needed to do to make this innovative—and necessary—investment happen.

"This was not a basic software program; this was a complex MRP system. We needed a whole team. One person was not going to be able to take on this huge undertaking," Marinaro explained. "That's when we engaged the program's creator, Sage, and industry consultants to get it up and running. We'd meet every day for months, trying to understand the terminology until we finally broke through."

Due to Bob's insistence to keep moving forward, X3 finally went live after three years of development. Today, the system has evolved to enable the company to automate the entire process, from ordering ingredients and producing meals to documenting final delivery to customers. The system fully integrates business functions and reporting through a series of modules, as well as ensures quality control checkpoints.

By 2008, with such processes in place, Whitsons had reached $100 million in annual sales, making it one of the 20 largest contract management firms in the country. That's when Whitsons began its second attempt to expand its prepared meals division into the retail arena. While the Whitcombs' initial foray into home-delivered meals may not ultimately have been successful, they had been dealing with other people's ideas and products.

Could a product of their own design be more bankable? Perhaps driven by their Christian desire to do good while also sensing the advent of a new trend, the team worked to create a line of gluten, casein, and soy-free meals called Nu-Life.

Launched in 2010, Nu-Life was targeted at the autism community because, at the time, many medical specialists believed that gluten, found in wheat, and casein, found in dairy products and soy, exacerbated the gastro-intestinal system and created an auto-immune response that can be connected to the symptoms of autism.

Although the Whitcombs were onto something with gluten-free meals, the company was ahead of the curve, and Nu-Life's focus was entirely too narrow to sustain sales. After about two years, the Whitcombs retrenched. But they still believed packaged meals were a market niche worth exploring, and over the next three to four years, the company would try creating private label meals for various supermarket chains, such as Wegman's and Stop 'n Shop.

The process was wearisome; Whitsons would sit down with a customer to design and cost out the meals to its specifications, only to learn that, in the interim, the client had changed their mind about the product. For Whitsons, it seemed like endless effort for almost no sales.

After about two frustrating years, the company closed the door on this opportunity, chalked the losses up to the cost of the learning curve, and plowed forward. However, this would ultimately bring them in contact with big-box retailer Walmart, with a request to develop a line of vacuum-sealed meals to market.

The deal with Walmart was fortuitous. It began with a phone call from a sales partner who had been asked by Walmart to find a company that could make exactly the kind of meals Whitsons had been experimenting with. Over several months of negotiations, Whitsons was able to create a two-tiered deal with the Bentonville, AR, giant.

First, Whitsons would produce and package a private-label line of 12 different meals for Walmart. Then, because Walmart wanted to test the strength of the paleo diet movement, Whitsons also developed six meals that it would produce and Walmart would sell under a brand Whitsons called Tastefully Plated. Tastefully Plated Paleo meals, which could be found in about 4,000 Walmart units, were one of three lines of Tastefully Plated meals; the others were called Originals and Naturals.

Peter Johnson, director of culinary, explained that it was one of the most complex research and development production projects the prepared meals division ever endured. In his 12 years with Whitsons, he had never experienced anything quite like it. Whitsons had to bring in new equipment like nitrogen tunnels, hold multiple meetings to perfect a single meal, troubleshoot the design process of a 6-sided box, and conduct high-end photo shoots.

"We went through rigorous testing on those products," Johnson said. "The photo shoots were actually pretty interesting, though. We went down to the Walmart Innovation Center, where they had individual prep rooms with pass-through windows, where you would put the food in this rotating window, and on the other side was the tasting room. Here, they could shut off the lights and essentially shut down all your other senses from being stimulated so you can focus on the taste of the food. Top-notch R&D."

Whitsons' deal with Walmart was "transformational," but the family believed that it was only the start. Fortunately, when you partner with a company the size of Walmart, word does get around, and other retailers began reaching out to Whitsons wishing to discuss similar deals.

As a result, Whitsons entered into a seven-store test with Target in several Long Island stores to sell its Tastefully Plated Naturals line. On the West Coast, the company signed a partnership with 7-Eleven to test the sale of Tastefully Plated Originals. Eventually, none of these retail opportunities panned out as expected, and the division had to switch gears once again.

"What came out of that experience—unplanned—was that we honed this great capacity for agility," said Bob. "We could change direction on a dime and do it at exceptional speed. And it wasn't just leadership making that decision. There was a willingness among the team—they took a holistic approach, and this outlook has made a difference in the longevity of the business. It's part of what's enabled us to get through these difficult times."

"We never said 'no,'" explains Koutras. "We looked at a request and asked, how could we make that work? We just found different ways to be successful where we could be—and where we weren't, we learned through that process."

Though the retail opportunities didn't materialize as anticipated, the family recognized that it had the capability to serve the nation's largest retailer and develop a line of meals that generated real demand, and that was quite an accomplishment. This was a pivotal moment for the prepared meals division, as it revealed so many untapped opportunities the company had yet to consider. They had certainly come a long way from an overnight, makeshift commissary at Kaufman Astoria Studios.

"I watched Whitsons and the family grow up," Torrez said as she reflected on all the transformations the company underwent through the turn of the millennium and beyond. "We only had one room and a manual sealer in Huntington, and now we have so much space and resources to try new projects. All the new machines and automation have made my job easier, and it is exciting.

"This company has a lot of opportunities for people to be supervisors or managers or get training and education. We had some ups and downs some years, but now, it's incredible to see how things have changed—for the better."

Those ups and downs Torrez referred to include the influx of management that came and went over a period of five years until they found the right leader for its prepared meals vision: Paul Burnup, who would finally lead this Whitsons division to new heights.

Now operating out of seven geographically dispersed culinary centers, prepared meals have grown to become an equally successful division of Whitsons, working in collaboration with contract management to offer a single-source solution that is unparalleled in the industry. With both major divisions thriving, Whitsons was ready to accept that there was a bigger future waiting out there than any of the original family members could have ever imagined.

10. A Call for Stewardship

With its contract management and prepared meals divisions built for a promising future, Whitsons found itself in a flux of positive growth and change. In 2009, the regional company once again gained national recognition. That year, the International Foodservice Manufacturers Association, a Chicago-based organization that represents much of the industry's supply chain, honored CEO Bob Whitcomb—and, by extension, the company—with a Silver Plate as Operator of the Year in the Foodservice Management category.

The Silver Plate Award, inaugurated in 1954, recognizes the top foodservice operators in nine categories—every segment from quick-service and full-service restaurants to hotels and specialty foodservice. With the honor, Bob joined foodservice's unofficial "hall of fame," a list that includes the CEOs of ARA Services (now Aramark), Sodexo, and Compass Group.

But as Whitsons continued to grow, the Whitcombs realized that they needed to rethink the organization's business model. The company still didn't have many of the established departments that a company of this size might be expected to have.

For example, up until that time, Whitsons had never had a purchasing department per se. Instead, one of the brothers had always been the de facto purchasing agent; for a time, John handled purchasing, and then Mike took over. Each man worked closely with Marinaro, who not only continued to input new products into the ever-growing database but also negotiated some purchasing contracts.

The Whitcombs soon realized that this practice would hobble the company's ability to grow. So they hired a consultant to come in and show them how to build a proper procurement department, as well as to help them find a person to run it.

Marinaro was part of the interview team primarily because he had worked so closely with vendors over the years that he understood how purchasing should work. He also demonstrated that he had the Whitcomb work ethic and do-it-yourself attitude—in more than just the IT department.

Case in point: During the famous Long Island blackout in 2005, Marinaro ordered fuel to be delivered the next day for the backup generator. However, the delivery man overfilled the generator, tripping the shut-off valve and leaving the office without power. Schettino went to Marinaro's home that weekend and left him a note, alerting him to the crisis.

When Marinaro saw the note, he literally ran to the office—still in his workout clothes. He and Mike worked together siphoning fuel from the generator to reduce the level to below the shut-off point. "I remember team members walking by, asking, 'Why is the IT guy pumping fuel?'" Marinaro said.

During the interviews with candidates for the purchasing director, one of Marinaro's questions was a simple one, but with major implications. He would ask each candidate whether he or she bought or leased their car. Whatever the answer, Marinaro's next question was: How did you negotiate with the car dealer?

"I learned from my father that you can't always take things at face value. You need to be able to analyze products to see what really goes into the cost of the item," said Marinaro, whose first experience in sales negotiation came as a teenager when his father took him to buy a Discman. The Discman retailed for $330, but Mr. Marinaro was able to purchase it for $180 by haggling with the store's owner.

Candidates came and went, but none of them were able to answer the negotiation question to the family or Marinaro's satisfaction.

Finally, the consultant said to the Whitcombs, "I give Michael an A in procurement. He should head procurement, and you should hire someone else to run Information Technology." The Whitcombs wisely took this advice, and since then, Marinaro has come full circle to lead both departments as vice president of supply chain and information technology.

During this same time, technology was at a turning point for the company. Witnessing the success of the X3 system in prepared meals operations, the school nutrition team recognized the importance of integrating its own process and reporting abilities. Under the direction of John, Kelly Friend, then IT director Gustavo Monne, John's daughter, Christine Rota, and an outside technological consulting firm, Fulcrum Digital, the development of a management information system known as Dine Central (now Culinary Suite) began.

"We had a lot more innovation on the technology front than we gave ourselves credit for, and Culinary Suite is the perfect example of that," said John. "We had all these systems that worked independently, but they didn't 'talk' to each other, making the administrative part of our growing business a challenge. We wondered if there was a system out there that would bring different processes together, like purchasing, nutrition, production, and reporting. There wasn't—so we built one."

Rota, who joined the company's culinary center operations in 2008, was appointed the Whitsons lead in developing Culinary Suite after demonstrating her skills in supporting X3 and other software applications. Over the better part of three years, the team worked diligently with Fulcrum Digital to create an automated system from scratch that would ultimately facilitate the flow of information between multiple business functions that were completed manually in the industry at the time.

Since Culinary Suite launched in 2016, the game for Whitsons has changed. Purchasing and commodity utilization are now prompted by a menu planning module that pulls menu options from a comprehensive recipe database of pre-approved ingredients and substitutions. These ordering efficiencies are further supported by digital inventory management and a two-way communication system with vendors. Functions also include menu customization by location, which further connects with an accredited analysis system to ensure meal pattern and nutritional compliance, as well as interface with another technological development, FDMealPlanner, to provide customers with access to mobile menus, nutrition, allergen information, and more.

What Whitsons has found to be most efficient about Culinary Suite's integrative prowess was its reporting abilities, which provide on-demand, transparent tracking for internal and external documentation and audit requirements.

"Once we trained the team and they understood the system, it created efficiencies we didn't even consider," said Rota. "It streamlined our supply chain process and helped control costs. It eliminated excess paperwork, which saved managers desk time so that they could focus on customer service more. Reporting was more accurate—we had real-time access to business metrics."

"Culinary Suite was the start of including more sophisticated technology in our operations," John explained. "We had other systems in place, such as Salesforce for customer management and NetChef for supply chain management, but we had only scratched the surface of the power of technology and how important a role it plays in service." Since that realization, the IT department has expanded and diversified to respond to ever-changing advances.

Legal and human resources departments at Whitsons also evolved over time, beginning with a part-time legal counsel: Corinne Kevorkian, who started with the company in 2010. Born in France to a French mother and an American father, Kevorkian decided as a teenager that she wanted to come to the U.S. and learn something about her father's homeland.

She graduated from Oberlin College in Ohio, taught French for a year, and then, influenced by the fact that her father was a lawyer, went to Boston College for her law degree. After earning her Juris Doctorate, Kevorkian worked for a couple of New York City law firms and as general counsel for Schumacher & Co., a global fabric manufacturer headquartered in Manhattan, before learning that Whitsons was looking for a lawyer.

"I thought it could be interesting," she recalled. "Schumacher also was a family business, fifth generation, so I understood that. And I'm one of seven kids. I met with Beth, Bob, and Doug, and there was a connection."

The Whitcombs hired Kevorkian to work three days a week, commuting from Manhattan. Within two years, she was working four days a week, and in early 2014, the Whitcombs asked her to join the leadership team and work full-time, heading the legal and HR departments.

Two of the women instrumental in leading the 9/11 efforts—Schettino and Norton—had been working in HR at the time before being assigned more specific tasks under Kevorkian. Norton, who joined the company in 2001 and had been sharing HR duties with Schettino, was named director of recruitment. A new position, director of workplace safety, was created for Schettino—a role designed to create programs to improve and make team members more aware of the importance of workplace safety. After establishing the new safety department, Schettino returned to her HR roots as the department's vice president.

Kevorkian has since retired, passing the legal reins to another accomplished law professional, Greg Robbins, whose 30 years of law firm and in-house corporate law experience in both New York and Connecticut has continued to elevate Whitsons' legal processes and facilitate acquisition opportunities. Whitsons was impressed with his background and knew he was the person to take the lead, having previously served as General Counsel to Veeco Instruments, a Long Island-based public company, for 20 years. Robbins found himself immediately at home with Whitsons.

"It was clear from the beginning that everything was about family. Paul and Beth were friendly and transparent. I didn't find there was a real acclimation period," recalled Robbins. "It was easy to get to know people. I didn't have to pretend or try to be anyone else. It was 'come and be yourself and do good work,' and that's the way it has been since day one. You're appreciated for who you are, and it works really well."

Robbins has since gone on to build the legal department to include new team members, standardized legal procedures, and qualified processes. Learning the foodservice industry and moving into new regions and markets has been a welcomed challenge, one that Robbins has met with exemplary skill, which he credits to the culture of Whitsons.

"What I've found unique is that Whitsons lets people grow into their natural capabilities," said Robbins. "They trusted me—a relatively new member of the team—to take a significant lead in their company growth. It's a really supportive environment, and I'm not sure that opportunities or faith in people are easily given in many other companies."

Whitsons' faith in Robbins was clearly well-founded. Since his start, he has been instrumental in the successful completion and integration of five acquisitions and acclimation to five new states (all with diverse governmental regulations and requirements). All of these changes to Whitsons' corporate infrastructure and business models were helping to set the stage for future growth.

***

By 2015, Whitsons hit what the family called "an inflection point." The older Whitcombs—Bill, Doug, Bob, and John—were either in or close to their 60s.

Inevitably, in a family business, the question must always be asked: Who is going to keep the company going after the older generation retires? As a company grows, it becomes tougher to manage: more team members, more business, more systems, and a more complicated organizational chart.

When everyone at the C-level wants to know what's going on everywhere, all the time, processes, and function begin to slow, gummed up by the executives' need to be in control.

This is often the point where, at many companies, the founders decide to step aside, find a buyer, and let new owners take the company to the next level. But the Whitcombs were not ready to take that path.

This was a proud and stubborn family, one that had built a company by defying the odds and never giving up, no matter the circumstances. They were not about to simply place what they had grown into strange hands and sail away. Fortunately, they didn't have to. What the Whitcombs possessed that many other families with businesses don't have was numbers.

Most "mom-and-pop" companies are literally that: a husband and wife create and grow the business, with a couple of young children who, as they grow to adulthood, may or may not want to continue that legacy. Or they are formed by two or three siblings who get together to seek their fortune, a partnership that may or may not work out over time.

But the Whitcomb children were nine, and as the oldest of them began to consider retirement, the youngest, Paul, was ready to take the helm. On June 4, 2015, he did just that, becoming, to borrow from the parlance of the technology world, Generation 1.5.

"One of the amazing things about the family and the business is that we all have different skills," explained Beth. "There is not a lot of overlap. On the flip side, there were five or six of us, each doing our own thing in a straight line and maybe not connecting. We decided it was time. Paul took over, and we all agreed that he would lead us and that we would all pull together. We've taken the cap off what we can achieve. We decided to get out of our own way."

Paul literally grew up in the family business. Born in 1971, he was not yet eight years old when the Whitcombs took over the Bon-Bon. As soon as he was able, he did whatever he could to help the business. When Whitsons began its vending program, Paul would help fill the machines.

As the company began to grow its contract management business, Paul would fill in as a substitute whenever and wherever was necessary. When he went off to college at Towson State University in Maryland, he kept his foodservice skills sharp by working in the university's catering department. And when he was off from school, he worked for Whitsons in its off-premise catering operations.

Still, Paul's first thought after graduation was not to join the business full-time but to make his own mark on the world. That notion was fleeting, however. It took only a little soul-searching for him to realize in his heart that he belonged with his siblings. However, during his first job with the firm, he might have been excused if he had considered changing his mind.

He got his start as an assistant manager at the Fresh Air

Fund Camp in Fishkill, NY. The Fresh Air Fund, founded in 1877 by a Pennsylvania minister named Willard Parsons, operates five camps on the Sharpe Reservation in Fishkill, bringing more than 3,000 New York City kids from low-income families for one- to two-week experiences away from the congestion of the inner city.

It was, to put it mildly, a tough environment for a 20-something. Living in a non-air-conditioned cabin with perhaps a dozen 9- to 12-year-old boys in the summer heat would not have been Paul's choice for indoctrination into the contract management business.

Despite the working conditions, however, Paul found that he enjoyed the job. Besides learning about volume food preparation, he developed a knack for placing food orders, something at which the camp's foodservice manager was not adept. Paul became skilled at breaking down meal counts, calculating portions, and ordering and organizing products.

He also discovered, "I'm a great No. 2 in the kitchen, and I loved the experience of making people happy through food."

After paying his dues in the field—sometimes literally—Paul moved into the corporate office. He worked in payroll for a while, helping to build systems for tracking items such as vacation time. Then, he began to work with brother Doug in sales. Here, he said, was where he felt most comfortable as a team member. He finally believed he was truly contributing to the family business.

For years, he went after school district accounts in New York and Connecticut, occasionally butting heads with those salespeople Whitsons would eventually hire. In 2012, Paul became executive vice president, where he remained until becoming CEO.

With Paul now in the top spot, the other brothers assumed new roles. John became the chief operating officer for the contract management division, while Bob became the COO of the prepared meals division. Doug took on the purchasing part of the business as chief product officer, and Mike was named vice president of customer relations, working with clients and Whitsons' on-site personnel to enhance the foodservice experience for all customers. Beth remained the CFO, Andy stayed on as executive chef, and Bill continued as director of fleet services.

However, the Whitcombs were smart enough to know

that they also needed to plan for the next generation, and they acknowledged to each other that this generation could not be as family-centric as the first.

There were two reasons for this: There were no guarantees how many of the Whitcomb children would want to follow in their parents' footsteps, and those who might have the desire certainly would not yet be old enough and experienced enough to lead the company.

As of 2024, there were several next-generation Whitcombs working in various aspects of the business, along with several spouses: IT, purchasing, marketing, shipping, operations, and accounting.

The initial "elders" of this small group were Craig, Doug's son, a regional vice president charged with establishing a company beachhead in the Tri-State area and growing business in that region, particularly in schools; Bill Jr., vice president of customer experience, who was the driving force behind Whitsons' school garden and community service initiatives; and Beth's daughter, Mary DiStefano, who earned her stripes in the marketing department and now leads as the senior marketing manager responsible for Whitsons' promotional efforts.

Craig and Bill were also key leaders in the Andrews gourmet catering division and corporate dining operations management before assuming their current roles.

Bob's son Robert Whitcomb, Jr. joined the purchasing team in 2009 and now serves as director of supply chain for our prepared meals division. Bob's other son, Ryan, worked as a registered dietitian in the nutrition department from 2012 to 2017 before venturing out to start his own wellness consulting firm.

Jean Whitcomb, Mike's wife, worked for many years in the accounting department as a controller and part-time as an auditor. John's daughter, Christine, who managed the development of Culinary Suite, has since been promoted to director of applications in the IT department.

Laurie's son, David Smith, began working in the logistics side of the prepared meals division in 2003 and has since advanced to vice president of culinary operations. Her daughter, Amanda

Smith, began supporting accounting in 2000 and now heads up the payroll department.

Mike Rota, Christine's husband, served as head of quality control and was responsible for USDA and FDA compliance until he left to join Nature's Bounty, a division of Nestlé. Tony DiStefano, Mary's husband, serves as director of strategic operations for residential and K-12 accounts.

While the next generation has certainly begun making its own mark on the future, many individuals outside of the family have also made a tremendous impact on the company's 45 years of success. What was once a small restaurant business had indeed grown to a formidable—yet somehow still humble—multi-million-dollar, multi-state contract management firm. It was clear that in order to preserve this legacy, the company needed to shift its perspective to one of longevity.

Recognizing that one day, this family business would outlast its original owners, the Whitcombs knew they needed to develop the next round of company leaders from among its extended family. And thus, the concept of company stewardship became a critical component of Whitsons' long-term business strategy: identifying those team members that will ultimately foster the Whitsons Way for generations to come.

"Finding the right team is the most difficult, yet the most important, part of stewardship," explained Paul. "People have to first understand our culture and history, and then they have to see their part in it. They have to be able to take what was given to them from those here before, leave their mark, and then pass that on to the next leader. That's the concept of stewardship we want to embrace—a legacy that outlives us, yet still embodies us at the same time."

The grooming of these stewards had been taking place for several years with people such as Fautas, Marinaro, and Gersbeck. But the best example of this stewardship has been Friend, the first person not a Whitcomb to reach the C-suite level. Hired more than three decades earlier, she had served in several capacities over the years as a unit manager, an internal marketer, a salesperson, an operations director, and a vice president.

She embraced her role as a family member and proved her natural leadership in so many ways over the years. So committed was she to Whitsons and the foodservice industry that she even studied to become a Certified Dietary Manager so she could better understand the nutritional aspects of menu development. Friend became John's choice to succeed him as COO of the contract management business, which she did in early 2016.

"In this role, I feel that I am an extension of what I helped build," said Friend. "I try to show people that there is so much potential here. There is tremendous value in keeping good talent and promoting from within, as is understanding where we came from, how we got here, and why this business is so important."

The contract management side of the business was now set to grow into a new era. Working closely with Gersbeck, Koutras, and Craig, Friend was determined to change Whitsons' reputation from just a regional "family" company to a veritable national competitor. The company never wanted to lose sight of its cultural uniqueness, but it was time to show the industry that Whitsons was more than ready to lead among the big players.

"It took a lot of learning curves to get where we are today," said Craig. "As we cut our teeth in school nutrition, we'd do so through trial and error. Now, under Kelly's focused leadership, we've refined a business process that allows us to compete at a high level and acquire clients aligned with who we are and what we value."

"No longer are we at the mercy of whoever is open to a change and willing to try us out," Friend added. "We have made our presence known, and our reputation precedes us. Because of the loyalty and passion of so many talented team members over the years, we never had to change who we are as a company. We're proud of our history and excited about where the future will lead us."

At the same time as Friend was taking over from John, the family decided to find someone to assume the reins of the prepared meals division from brother Bob.

The new team member would be responsible for assessing the institutional side of the business and determining whether the people and the infrastructure are solid enough to grow the business. The company was in the process of designing a larger production facility in New Jersey that would enable the company to consolidate operations from Queens and Elizabeth, NJ, to enable the company to grow.

After bringing in an executive from the outside to manage the division, which failed to work out, Whitsons turned inward again to a longtime executive with knowledge of and experience with both the contract and the production side. Fautas returned to the prepared meals team in mid-2017.

"The reality was, Chris was logically the right person for the job," said Paul. "While he fit seamlessly with contract management, he had the ability to understand prepared meals, and that was an important element."

Fautas was able to stabilize the business and bring much-needed direction back to the team. But soon, Fautas was needed back in contract management, leaving the prepared meals role vacant. What came next was unexpected—and David Smith was quick to point out what exactly went wrong.

"We struggled to find the right person whose experience and values aligned with ours," he said. "Unfortunately, not every leader we hired turned out to be the best fit, even if seemingly qualified. To take this division to where we envisioned it, we learned we had to look beyond the resume credentials and also consider a candidate's mindset, passion, and ability to deliver on their promises."

And he would know—as a next-generation family member who grew up in the prepared meals division and now leads as its vice president of operations, Smith was familiar with the caliber of management it took to run a business of this size and complexity.

That's when the company met the current chief operating officer of prepared meals, Paul Burnup—though the path to Whitsons for Burnup wasn't cut and dried. During the initial interview process, it came down to Burnup and another candidate, but at the time, the majority of Whitsons' leadership voted in favor of the one with the most C-suite level experience.

"Paulie was clearly an excellent operational leader, but we thought we needed more of an executive leader, and so we selected the other person," Paul Whitcomb explained. "But we never forgot the impact he made on us: he has a go-get-it, can-do attitude that really fit in well with our culture. I believed we just needed to find the right opportunity for him."

Luckily for Burnup and Whitsons, it didn't take long to bring them back to the table. In fact, Burnup had simply reached out later that year to wish the family a Merry Christmas—at the same time, Paul was planning to contact him after determining, to their frustrated dismay, that their current leader wasn't meeting expectations. But, at the time, Burnup was making headway at another major competitor—would he even want to make the move to Whitsons after being initially turned down?

"There was no question in my mind that I had a natural connection with Paul and his vision of where he wanted his company to be," Burnup states. "I saw the potential and just knew I wanted to be a part of that growth.

"I've worked for large corporations before, but Whitsons was noticeably different. I felt an instant camaraderie with leadership and a mutual sense of trust. I wanted to be a part of this unique culture and play a role in leading the company in new directions.

"It wasn't a choice for me. I knew I belonged here."

For Whitsons, it was also a no-brainer. Burnup had extensive experience in leading and transforming foodservice environments. But, before they could pull the trigger, the infamous COVID-19 pandemic hit. Burnup was hired—but his first task would be to help Whitsons execute its COVID response, during which time, he quickly proved his prowess for developing a team and efficiently operating in a demanding environment.

Combined with his background in operations, financial savviness, and implementing continuous improvement control standards, Burnup had a knack for identifying and developing opportunities for growth. Whitsons realized they had finally found the right fit for the prepared meals division. It was clear that his ambition was matched by his ability, with a genuine commitment to cultivating the Whitsons Way culture among his team and the company at large.

And so, shortly after joining Whitsons, Burnup was escalated to the role of vice president and, eventually, chief operating officer of prepared meals.

Subic recounted the difficult path between Fautas' and Burnup's leadership. "There were honestly periods when it was challenging because of the management situation. What kept me going through what I call the 'dark times' was the support from my team and from Chris, who, even though he had since returned to schools, would still be there to encourage me to hang in there, to keep going and it will change for all the better. Then what our team now calls the 'Paulie B era' began, and excitement for us grew again."

"Once Paulie arrived, everything pivoted," Smith said. "We returned to our roots. We started going back to our strengths—supporting the K-12 market, the senior population, and other community programs. From there, we were able to realistically look at what new opportunities would fit into our business model."

"Paulie saw everyone's potential—he knew who he could count on to help him take this part of the company to the next level," added Subic, who was immediately recognized as a higher-level leader and poised to support the division alongside Burnup and Smith.

"We went through a cultural evolution. You can see on the faces of the people that they take ownership. They don't come in and do their eight hours and that's it. They work together well and are proud of what they do and how they do it. People really care. They are putting love into these meals that are a sustenance for someone else. With the right team and attitude, we knew we could accomplish anything together."

But no one could predict just how much they would be able to accomplish under the new leadership in such a short amount of time.

"K-12 business was a significant market for the prepared meals team at the time I joined, but now it has become a critical service sector," Burnup noted. "Then, when we pursued acquisitions, we discovered even more possibilities. We've realized the power of being a one-source solution: we're combining our strengths in on-site management and prepared meals to offer a blended service that not many others can provide."

As Paul explained it: "If you're a contract management company, you become an expert at that. If you're a prepared meals company, you become an expert at that. We are in the unique position as an expert at both. That's a competitive edge that's going to lead the industry in a whole new direction, and our team is ready for it."

***

As Whitsons has grown as a company, the Whitcombs' extended family has grown as well—and there are quite a few veterans at Whitsons. Relatives of team members have also joined the firm, such as Karen Gersbeck, wife of John Gersbeck. Beginning shortly after John as a district manager, Karen has found a niche supporting the New England team as a senior human resources business partner.

"It's been amazing to witness the growth from when I first started until now. Who knew that this New York-centric business would change the industry one meal at a time and become a dominant leader? I feel honored to have been a part of that development all these years."

Fautas' son Marc joined the firm and worked in various roles within the prepared meals division for a number of years, eventually learning the business inside and out. Marc served as depot manager and, eventually, production manager.

Marc remembered fondly how Bob took him under his wing when he was hired, as well as when he job-shadowed Mike for a year. When Bob's son, Rob, joined Whitsons, Marc mentored him "just as his dad had done for me."

Other veterans have shared their experiences over the years. Original Hicksville team member Gertrude Duca once proudly recalled how it felt to be Whitsons' very first school district account.

"Hicksville High School became Whitsons' show account, and school districts came from all over Long Island to see what we had to offer our students for lunch. We all made sure every station looked its best. They would even bring some students, and they'd all be amazed at how different we were. Doug personally coming to our account and congratulating us was so meaningful.

I was so proud to know that I was part of that team that helped Whitsons to get its start in school lunch—and I stayed there until my retirement. They were my second family."

Lisa Torrez credits her 24 years at Whitsons with how comfortable she feels in her "work home." She explained how she has always felt special from the moment she was interviewed. In fact, knowing she had very little English-speaking skills at the time, Mike tried to hire her by speaking Spanish—failing miserably, she noted, but making Torrez smile with appreciation to know he tried.

"Mr. Robert," as she affectionately called Bob, also holds a special place in her heart. "Mr. Robert is like a father to me. He did everything for me. Always helping me. I was so sad when he retired. Everyone here is really my family."

However much the Whitcombs might think of team members as family, as the company expanded in size, geography, and staff, the Whitcombs were, in a sense, becoming more distant from their team members. They had always believed that Whitsons' team members were the key to the company's continued success and had always given them the chance to grow and make a difference within the company.

But when a company grows from 300 team members to 5,000 and branches out to 12 more states, it becomes difficult to keep in touch with individual employees. Another organization might chalk it up to inevitable growth, but Whitsons remained steadfast in its commitment to family values.

They established the typical corporate recognition programs, team member events, and "Town Hall" communications to keep the company as close together as possible. But there was nothing more personally significant and profound for the Whitcomb family than the creation of its Whitsons Family Foundation.

In 2010, when a district manager came to them with a sad story about a struggling single mother who was upset that she didn't have any money to buy her children presents for Christmas, Whitsons did not brush aside the anecdote with a "not my problem" attitude.

That was not how the Whitcombs had been raised, and they

were not about to let the company's size get in the way of their calling as Christians. The Whitcombs decided to "pass the hat," as it were, and raised about $1,500 for the family. Paul recalled that the gesture was "life-changing for the mother. A few dollars from a few people changed an event for her and her children in a small but very real way."

This act started a conversation among the executives about how many other team members might be in similar straits. By asking district managers their opinions, they came up with a list of about a dozen more people, and the company helped these families as well. This convinced the Whitcombs that there was an ongoing need and that they had a Christian duty to respond.

So they created the Whitsons Family Foundation, seeding it with $50,000 and promising to match, dollar for dollar, voluntary employee contributions. Formed as a 501C non-profit charity, the Foundation is available to any team member or their families. The Whitcomb family members are the trustees of the foundation, and there are no administrative costs; all the money donated is used to honor requests. Moreover, all requests that come in are redacted anonymously before presentation to the committee so that the merit of each case is weighed objectively.

"This was a defining moment for me personally," shared Bill, who was fully behind the charitable endeavor. "The creation of the Whitsons Family Foundation is something I am extremely proud of. How we've helped our team members through some deeply challenging times has been extraordinary, a true embodiment of our mission."

The grant money has helped victims recover from the devastation of a fire, ease the burden of costly medical treatments, and cover the cost of books for a college student. It has aided multiple hurricane victims, grieving loved ones, and simply good people just struggling to pay their electric bills in an inflated society.

"I will never forget the phone call that broke my heart and put me in tears," recalled Dee, who was the first administrator of the Foundation. She shared how she had both the privilege and the burden of concealing the identities of applicants and then sharing the results with them.

"I had called one woman to let her know that she would be receiving a check, and I could hear the relief in her heart as she called me an angel and cried that I was saving her life. I couldn't take any credit for it, but there is no greater feeling in the world than knowing you were a part of something that changed someone's life and gave them hope."

It is not only recipients who are touched by the awards. One foodservice director for a Long Island school district, who had applied for the money on behalf of two of her employees, penned this letter to the Foundation in 2012:

> *"I would like to take this time to thank you for your help with my team members in the aftermath of Hurricane Sandy. The day before Thanksgiving break, I received a very heartfelt and gracious phone call from one of the applicants. She stated she would now be able to have Thanksgiving dinner, even without heat or water. Amid the chaos, with most of her belongings outside her home, a FedEx truck arrived with a check for her.*
>
> *"Although I was aware of the Foundation, it wasn't until this past experience that I was able to take advantage of this wonderful benefit and to experience how it could make such a difference to a fellow Whitsons team member in need."*

Over a decade later, the Foundation is still helping team members through difficult times. It is among one of the most profound and meaningful humanitarian efforts the family has endeavored to give back to those who dedicate so much to them day in and day out.

"Doing the right thing, day in and day out, year after year, is what defines us and what I'm most proud of," said Paul. "It's the little things—both in life and at work—that add up to form the big picture."

It's a big picture that has been over 45 years in the making. With a strengthened focus on stewardship and the future, the Whitcombs intended to honor the calling that started with their mother and father.

And when the world changed unexpectedly due to a global pandemic, it became evident once again that Whitsons was not just in the service business but a servant of the people in their communities.

Whitsons' Senior Leadership Team

1998

Top Row: Andy, Mike, Paul, John, Laurie
Bottom Row: Doug, Beth, Bob, Gina

2024

Top Row: Beth Bunster, Rishma Verma, Greg Robbins, Paul Burnup, Kelly Friend, Mike Marinaro, Miles Williams, Ozzie Orsillo

Bottom Row: Lloyd Trotter, Paul Whitcomb, Daphne Dufresne

**All photos from family and company archives

11.
COVID-19: A Time for Change

By 2020, there was no longer any doubt among the family that the company had a stable future. They had faith that Whitsons would continue to be a pillar for the long haul. The company was expanding into new territories, building more culinary centers, and diversifying its product lines and services.

They were leading the industry by exceeding nutritional regulations in their meals. Purchasing and nutrition teams painstakingly researched the best possible ingredients, free of harmful preservatives, artificial colorings and flavorings, trans fats, and other unsavory additions long before the Healthy Hunger Free Kid Act was instated in 2010—and continued to refine ingredients with a focus on supporting local and regional farms.

Whitsons also developed a number of garden programs to both support local sustainability and create awareness for their educational customers. On-site gardens were used for teaching and for incorporating fresh herbs and produce into the menu. Some clients elected to have greenhouses, and others grew vertical garden kits in their kitchens. But the fact remained that "homegrown" foods were an important part of the Whitsons' sustainability model.

Then, there was the world at large: Whitsons was expanding its mindset to address global environmental concerns. As one of 23 original organizations that joined the USDA's and EPA's initiative as US Food Loss and Waste 2030 Champions, they declared their commitment to do their part to help the nation reach its food loss and reduction goal.

This included pledging concrete steps to reduce waste in their operations by 50 percent by the year 2030, such as eliminating polystyrene and plastic salad containers, using biodegradable trays, and replacing plastic straws with paper ones. Share table programs, donating leftover food to local shelters, food pantries, meal programs, hormone and pest-free practices, and other conservation efforts continue to be at the forefront of service.

Not only was Whitsons progressing in time with the future of food and service, but their family was growing in ways they never expected. Team members from all over the company were embedding themselves into their communities and playing an active role in the growth and development of the business. Senior leadership included more than Whitcomb family members, and the industry was recognizing them as hospitality frontrunners.

With as much positive growth and success as Whitsons was building, it didn't mean that the company wouldn't continue to be tested. And they were, in 2020—but this time, the entire world was challenged right along with them. The hurdle was tiny yet dangerously alarming: a virus that became known as COVID-19.

There was an inkling that Whitsons' services might come in handy early in March when Westchester County, NY, went into lockdown. (The city of New Rochelle was considered "ground zero" for COVID-19 in New York state.) On March 16, New York City Mayor Bill DeBlasio closed all city schools.

Two days later, New Jersey Governor Phil Murphy ordered the closure of all schools in the state, and the following day, New York Governor Andrew Cuomo followed suit. That same day, Mike received a call from an official in New York City's Office of Emergency Management (OEM).

"I can't remember the exact request," recalled Mike, "But they said they wanted a meal box, you know, 12 or 15 meals per box, and they ordered 33,000. We thought they meant meals, so we divided that by 12 or 15 and said, not too bad, so we put them together and sent them out. Mid-delivery, they said, 'This is great. When are you shipping the rest of them?' That's when we realized they really wanted 33,000 meal boxes—450,000 meals—so we pulled everyone in for the weekend and churned them out."

Over the next month, OEM would place five orders, totaling more than 2.8 million meals. Paul and Doug secured a warehouse in Ronkonkoma, NY, which became a temporary base of operations. One month later, they negotiated a temporary lease on a refrigerated warehouse in Hauppauge, NY, from which Whitsons began production on May 3.

There was a period of chaos in which various entities didn't know exactly what they would need. For example, an emergency services unit would call and ask for 1000 meals, then call two hours later and increase the amount to 10,000 meals —only to revise that number again only a couple of hours after that.

It had been nearly 20 years since Whitsons handled a request of this magnitude, and that was also for New York City—on September 11, 2001. But while the surge of meals in the aftermath of 9/11 was limited both in scope and length, this latest emergency program was more far-reaching and would last for several months.

Beginning with shelf-stable meals and eventually expanding to fresh meals as well, the program would last well into October 2020. As if the program's size wasn't challenging enough, Whitsons faced an obstacle it never had to deal with in 2001: supply chain issues.

"We were working seven days a week, 14 to 17 hours a day, for that entire period," said Paul. "It was all about getting the sourcing down, coordinating teams, getting people in, finding locations, and distribution. Finding supplies at that point was hard, so we worked with some partners to accomplish that. It was crazy, but it was exhilarating at the same time."

At the end of April, OEM awarded Whitsons a contract to prepare and deliver ten million fresh and shelf-stable meals over the next three months. As the process worked itself into a routine, the company settled on two types of meal boxes—one shelf-stable and the other fresh—of a three-day supply of breakfast, lunch, and dinner. Between those meals and bulk deliveries, Whitsons was distributing about 400 pallets of food a day, or more than 20 tractor-trailers worth.

As the fall of 2020 progressed and the need for meal boxes

began to wane, Whitsons expanded its ability to provide emergency food relief by working with the US Department of Agriculture to deliver 1.1 million boxes of fresh meat, produce, milk, cheese, and vegetables to residents in five states through the Farmers-To-Families program: New York, New Jersey, Connecticut, Massachusetts, and Pennsylvania.

Over the ensuing 60 days, Whitsons would ship out some 34 million pounds of food. As of January 2021, the company had prepared and/or delivered 52.4 million pounds of food—4,000 truckloads—and logged 265,000 miles in those trucks. More than 2.6 million families benefited from the delivery of 29 million meals before the world would gravitate back toward "normal service."

For the Whitcombs, both the past "failures" the company had endured and their desire to be of faithful service to the larger community began to take on a new significance. They were building blocks for what would follow. Whitsons had created a reputation for itself as a firm that could pivot on a dime and alter its style of service in a New York minute. And so, their emergency services division was born in response.

Not only that, but the challenges that the COVID pandemic brought on further solidified Whitsons as a company.

"At a time when most of the world was forced to stay home, Whitsons once again showed its resilience," said Burnup. "Our team—both in prepared meals and the contract management side—didn't want to just stay home and do nothing. It gave people the resolve to not give up. It inspired them to help so many in their communities who were struggling to eat daily, let alone three times a day.

"Whitsons couldn't—wouldn't—shutdown. People needed us. It was a rallying point for the company as a whole. We were one company with a common goal: feeding the world and getting each other through this time."

Paul agreed, noting that it was Whitsons' natural response to face adversity head-on.

"No matter what's in front of us, we'll find our way. And we may be successful or we may not be, but either way, there's a lesson there, and it always makes us better."

***

It was also during this chaotic, unknown time that the family simultaneously joined the world in self-reflection. The elder siblings were at a precipice: do they continue building the vision that their parents began in 1979, or do they step back? Bob and his brothers and sister knew the time had finally come: they had a decision to make.

"COVID made us re-evaluate our lives. We were all impacted personally. People we knew were dying from this pandemic. Things we took for granted—good health, freedom, gatherings with family and friends—were taken from us without warning," Bob recalled.

"It was time for us to consider passing the torch. If—when—this crisis ended and things went back to 'normal,' we wanted our lives to be different. We spent the entirety of it building a business; a business we are proud of. But now, it was time to reap the rewards of a life hard worked. To treasure family time with grandchildren, to explore hobbies long put aside, and to make the most of every precious moment God grants us."

And so, Bob, along with brothers Bill, Doug, John, Mike, and Andy, sought the path of retirement. Paul and Beth, the youngest of the siblings, were already in place and willing to continue to lead the company forward.

Indeed, there was a lot to consider behind the decision to retire, including the current and future stability of the business. One of the challenges any company faces is growth. Whether organic or through acquisition, as a company becomes larger, growth becomes more difficult. So, while some members were ready to step down, company expansion was just about to rev up—and that required serious discussions about how to transition successfully.

As Bob explained it: "The more you grow your business, the more your receivables inevitably are. Consequently, you must secure an ever-increasing line of credit, and so on. It would limit the way we could grow and how much we could grow."

Ultimately, there comes a time when a company has a choice: Find a partner or become the prey of a larger, more well-financed fish.

"Partnerships" typically can be formed in one of two ways: Take the company public and sell stock to raise the necessary capital or turn the firm over to a partner, such as a venture capitalist, who will allow the company to operate as before, while providing the funds to allow the firm to continue its growth.

In the fall of 2021, Whitsons made the latter decision. It entered an agreement with GenNx360 Capital Partners, a minority-owned private equity firm based in New York City. GenNx360 would become a majority partner, and in return, Whitsons would continue to operate as before, with Paul as CEO and Beth as CFO—only now with the availability of additional resources to help with the company's growth.

In a statement to Whitsons' team members after a conference call in which the partnership was announced, Paul shared his excitement about the company's next phase with GenNx360. He wanted everyone to understand that the private equity firm was not going to change the company culture or dynamics. They were simply focused on investing in companies with proven and sustainable business models, like Whitsons. Their interest was expanding within our industry with the objective of accelerating growth—not micromanaging the successful formula already in place.

"GenNx360's investment in Whitsons will enable us to focus on driving our mission of Enhancing Life One Meal at a Time™," Paul explained to the team. "We will continue to build our team and our services and expand our reach to serve more communities wholesome and delicious meals. There will be no changes to our day-to-day management and operations, and the Whitcomb family will remain actively involved in the business."

Bob explained that the company spent quite some time searching for the right firm with whom to partner before settling on GenNx360. Founded in 2005 by investment banker Ronald E. Blaylock and former GE Vice Chair Lloyd Trotter, GenNx360 did more than just provide Whitsons with a solid financial backer; it set the stage for the next generation of opportunity as a minority-owned business with unlimited possibilities ahead of them.

Whitsons' current Board of Directors, which still includes Paul and Beth, had the background, resources, and vision to drive the company's mission forward. Diverse leadership enabled Whitsons to provide a service and product that is aligned with the multicultural world we live in and the ever-changing environments and adapts to unique customer population preferences.

"When I first heard about Whitsons, I remember how the themes of wholesome foods, family values, and personalized service stood out as differentiators from other companies I had worked with over the years," said Daphne Dufresne, GenNx Managing Partner and Whitsons' Chair of the Board. "As time went on and our partnership flourished, I no longer just 'heard' about these ideals; I now see them, feel them, and believe them as part of the family myself."

These ideals are upheld as Whitsons continues to raise its own bar. Their recent efforts include progressing as a 2030 US Food Loss and Waste Champion to reduce its carbon footprint on the planet and actively partnering with organizations such as Baylor Collaborative's Hunger Outreach Program Empowerment (HOPE) Team to combat food insecurity in the communities they serve.

Today, the company's vision is stewarded by its seasoned Senior Leadership Team (SLT), comprised of Paul, Beth, Kelly Friend, Ozzie Orsillo, Michael Marinaro, Greg Robbins, and Paul Burnup, who work in conjunction with the Board of Directors to strategically plan and executive company initiatives.

"This is a team dedicated to taking the best of Whitsons and moving it forward," said Paul. "We're laying the foundation for future generations—whether a Whitcomb leads it or not—to uphold the values of our organization and, essentially, make the world a better place through food, family, and service.

"If people can connect with our Whitsons Way culture and join us in living our mission, then that will be the true indicator that we fulfilled our father's wish of keeping our family together while also serving others."

The senior-level executives are also supported by a select group of management professionals designated as its Whitsons Leadership Team—future leaders tasked with developing and fulfilling Whitsons' culture, vision, and long-term goals. Among this next wave of leaders are next-generation Whitcombs, veteran team members, and rising stars who all embody Whitsons Way.

For it is the entirety of what Whitsons Way stands for—a commitment to food, family, and service—that is the legacy the family wants to leave behind. While the business itself is certainly one expression of it, what's most important to the Whitcombs are the people who have touched the lives of others through this spirit.

It's simply who Whitsons is—and who they will always be.

A Moment in Time

A distinguished family man adds one last framed photograph from his desk to his box of possessions; possessions that have accumulated in his office over the last 40-something years. A smile fills his heart as he looks at each one: the growth of his family from babies to adults, the honorable awards bestowed upon his company, and the books that shaped the course of his career. Each a treasured memory he will hold onto for as long as he lives.

What a bittersweet moment this is for him, reflecting on a rich past while letting it go to step into the future—his and that of his cherished family's company.

With pride, he takes a look around the place he's called his second home for most of his lifetime. This is where the magic happened. Where innovative ideas continued long after the company's inception. Where divergent sibling perspectives converged into promising strategies. Where team members came to laugh, share, cry, and make a difference. Where a mother would come to see all her children thriving together in one place.

While he looks at his father's reflection in the lobby plaque honoring the man who started it all, he quietly thinks to himself:

"We did it, Pop."

They did, indeed. Elmer and Gina Whitcomb bought a restaurant, and their children turned it into a legacy.

Epilogue: A Family's Reflection

In April of 2024, the month of the 40th anniversary of Elmer Whitcomb's death, members of the Whitcomb family reflected on their father's legacy, what the ensuing years have meant for the family, and what the future might hold.

If there was a common thread running through their thoughts, it was faith: faith in themselves, faith in each other, and, most importantly, faith that a higher power had helped to guide them along their decades-long path to success.

For Bob, the failure of the restaurants was more than just a learning experience for the family.

"It became the vehicle through which we were to be transformed," Bob said. "It would allow us to grow physically and spiritually. It was a process of encountering difficulties and overcoming them, and then moving on. It was us not giving up but persisting and becoming renewed and stronger because life will continue to deal with these challenges. There was a weariness that accompanied this," he added. "But there also was strength, wisdom, and spiritual comfort."

Mike agreed. "I am tremendously proud of how our company has grown, not only in size or in services but, more importantly, that our growth has remained faithful to what our dad believed in. It's something neither I nor my siblings have ever forgotten. It's written in our DNA."

As the eldest, Bill sees what his dad's true vision was and could not be more impressed with how it succeeded. "The growth of our company has been remarkable—but I am even more proud that we've never lost sight of our roots as a family. That's exactly what Pop wanted for us."

Paul said he has reflected on his parents' original decision to buy the restaurants "many times" over the years and has decided the move came down to a matter of "faith and trust."

"I know that their faith and trust in God played a big role in that decision," Paul said. "Faith that God has created each of us with a specific purpose and trust that wherever His will leads us, it is the best place for us to be."

Andy's vision of possibilities has never wavered. "I see Whitsons continuing to be dominant in the industry. We have always acted like a leader, not a follower. Adaptability and faith have been the key to our success and our strength so far. We have proven several times over our ability to stay sharp in the midst of chaos and change course in a heartbeat. At our core, we never doubted what could be possible."

Beth's philosophy is that life is a series of trials designed to make people better versions of themselves.

"Looking back, it is clear to me that life is actually a forging process, meant to make us into the people God intended," she explained. "I have found that the greatest gifts resulted from going through the darkest times. Faith is the only thing that gives me the strength to make it through.

"It is my greatest hope that I have helped my children build a strong foundation, strong enough to take them through their greatest struggles—which are certain to come—and gain strength and a deepening faith in the process."

So faith in God, combined with trust in the family structure, has led the Whitcombs and their company to this point—and helped their families to grow, as well. This is John's belief:

"At its core, Whitsons is a family business; a business with tight family relationships. A family that, as a unit, never quit, even when, by rights, we should have. A family that never gave up, even when all hope seemed lost. I believe that same tenacious stubbornness was a critical trait in raising our families successfully, too. And when that alone wasn't enough for a given situation, God would step in and alter our perspectives, yielding a better result."

And now that faith has brought the Whitcombs to the next chapter in their professional lives, with a partner that supports the company's vision for continued growth.

"It's an exciting time because the longevity of the business is clear," said Paul. "It's not going to change because I'm not here or any of my other siblings aren't here. It's going to keep going because of the whole Whitsons family. We've gotten to where we are in the hardest way possible, and we've done it in one of the most competitive marketplaces in the country. There is so much more opportunity out there, and we will find a way to capitalize on it."

John admitted that he was surprised by Whitsons' growth.

"I never envisioned that Whitsons would one day grow to its current market position and have the success the company now enjoys," he said. "Whitsons now has a large enough business presence to be a force in the industry for generations to come.

"While some of the original partners have wound down their business careers, we did so with the knowledge that the company was firmly positioned in the markets it served. Each market has significant growth potential. The core business of Whitsons is within highly evolved and stable markets, ones that remain unaffected by economic downturn."

Beth believes that the company's success is guaranteed in large measure because of the people the Whitcombs have hired over the years.

"Our company is stacked with talented people at all levels, all committed to Whitsons' success," she explained. "If we, the family, allow our team the freedom to take risks, Whitsons will grow at a much faster pace than in the past. This, in turn, will create more opportunities for our team to shine."

That in itself is a testament to how the Whitcomb family has grown since their father bought those two diner-like restaurants in Garden City in 1979. They have morphed from a group of blood relatives who managed a fledgling firm by the seat of their collective pants into the nucleus of an extended family of team members, each one as vital to the company as any one of the Whitcomb siblings.

Doug summed it up best when he lovingly reflected on the man who started this bold journey. "Now that I am a father myself, I finally realize the extent of the sacrifices Pop made to care for his family. I'm glad we took his dream, made our own sacrifices, and set the course for future generations. Now it's up to our extended family, related and honorary, to carry on the legacy we pass to them. I hope Dad is proud of what we've built together."

Elmer Whitcomb would indeed be proud.

About the Authors

Paul King is a journalist who has covered the foodservice industry for more than 40 years. During that time, he has worked at *Food Management, Nation's Restaurant News,* and *FoodService Director*. In 2015, he became a freelance writer, continuing to write about the foodservice industry. In addition to his work in the industry, Paul has crafted a second career as an amateur historian. A native of Pittsburgh, PA, in 2020, he released his first book, *Iconic Pittsburgh: The City's 30 Most Memorable People, Places & Things,* published by The History Press. A follow-up titled *Colorful Characters of Pittsburgh* was published in October 2023.

Jenny Dee is a multi-genre author with diverse professional experience of over 26 years in marketing, communications, and entrepreneurialism. Her first book, *Butterfly Travels*, was published in 2014. She has since released a mystery-romance trilogy (*The Lost Heritage Trilogy*), multiple children's books (*Meet the Z Team; Meri-Rose and the Four-Leaf Clover*), a humorous online dating memoir (*Dear Bumbling Boy*), and a poignant fictional abuse novel written to enlighten and empower survivors to thrive (*Beat Me With Your Words*). Her current and upcoming books can be found on Amazon and at *www.jennydeeauthor.com.*

Made in the USA
Middletown, DE
24 June 2024